QUINOA

Flakes, Flour & Seeds

RENA PATTEN

QUINOA

Flakes, Flour & Seeds

RENA PATTEN

Contents

Introduction

I am thrilled to have the opportunity once again to show the many wonderful and beneficial ways to use quinoa, known as a super grain (though it is a seed) and a superfood (which it is).

Since my first book *Cooking with Quinoa* followed by *Quinoa for Families* and *Everyday Quinoa*, I have been absolutely amazed how the interest in this tiny highly nutritionally-packed seed has grown to a level where you now find it included as an ingredient in many recipes.

The world has truly embraced this tiny seed and the nutritional and unique health benefits it has to offer.

For those who are just learning about quinoa, welcome to a diet that will be healthy, full of nutrients and delicious. And for those who are already the converted, this book will add to your recipes but in a slightly different way as I show you how to prepare more delicious easy to prepare recipes in four easy-to-read chapters showcasing how to use quinoa as a seed, as flakes, as flour and in its puffed form.

I still get quite overwhelmed at the amount of positive feedback that I get from so many people. They tell me how they have embraced the whole concept of adding quinoa to their daily diet regardless of whether they need to or have to do so and how much they appreciate the huge health benefits they get when they do.

It is really heart warming to hear repeatedly from people who have my previous books how these books have helped them become aware of the many different ways that quinoa can be prepared in the everyday kitchen and how much their health and that of their family has improved for the better since including it in their diet.

Many had no previous knowledge of quinoa and their initial introduction has been through their medical practitioner, dietician or naturopath who suggested they include quinoa in their daily diet. Quinoa is the perfect food if you are gluten/wheat intolerant.

There are people from all walks of life who for one reason or another, need to or just want to change their eating habits to benefit their health. It may be because they have been diagnosed with (or who already have) a certain health issue where diet seems to play a very important role. Or it may be people that have been looking for a general alternative to eating rice and pasta and claim to be able to better manage and control their weight by changing to and continuing to use quinoa.

And then, of course then there are people that eat quinoa simply because they like it.

When I wrote my first quinoa cookbook, my main purpose for doing so was to bring awareness of the existence of this seed and particularly the health benefits associated with it and to show the different ways that it can be used in your cooking.

A lot of people were not even aware that you could get quinoa in any other form other than as a seed.

I was also so surprised and dismayed to hear from those who were sprinkling quinoa seeds as is (without cooking) on their breakfast cereal. They were doing so as they were told they should be eating it. I was not surprised to hear that they did not find eating quinoa 'raw' very palatable. My quinoa cookbooks have now changed all of that.

It is really a very useful ingredient to use particularly when cooking for a group of people with varied dietary needs.

I have used quinoa in seed, flake, flour or puffed form as a main ingredient in all the recipes in this book to show how easy it is to replace grains such as wheat and rice.

I want to show you that you can create delicious tasting and more nutritional meals using quinoa in its four different forms and that you don't have to add products containing gluten/wheat for recipes to work or taste good.

As with all recipes in general, feel free to interchange ingredients such as herbs and spices to suit your taste or their availability in your kitchen at the time of cooking.

Recipes should be used as guides—you don't have to follow them precisely—except for baking when there needs to be a balance between the dry and wet ingredients.

I have also used common everyday ingredients that are readily available at your local supermarket or greengrocer.

I tend to use canned legumes and pulses a lot as I find them so easy and convenient and I always have some on hand in my pantry as I do some frozen vegetables in my freezer. I am rarely organized enough to know well in advance that I will need to soak legumes or pulses for 24 hours before I use them, hence the use of the canned variety. I must say though, the green grocer is my favorite shop and I always get so excited when I see all that beautiful fresh produce.

This book has something for everyone—it covers recipes for vegetarians, meat, seafood and poultry eaters.

I think it would be fair to say that we all have or know someone in our lives that has some special dietary need. Whether that someone is a family member, a friend, or a friend of a friend; whether it is an intolerance to wheat or gluten, an allergy or they are vegetarians or vegan, this cookbook will help you accommodate most dietary needs with tasty and easy-to-prepare meals designed to cater for everyone using ingredients that are inexpensive and readily available.

My philosophy in food has always been that people with special dietary requirements should not miss out and should be able to enjoy most of the food that people without special dietary requirements enjoy.

With quinoa and knowledge of the many different ways that it can be prepared, people can do just that.

What is quinoa?

Quinoa (pronounced keen-wah) is not a grain though many refer to it as one. Quinoa is a seed and not just any seed—it is considered to be an almost complete food, It is very high in protein, full of vitamins, totally free of gluten, wheat and cholesterol, usually organic and of great benefit to anyone's diet. It is very easy to prepare and tastes delicious.

In a nutshell, quinoa is a complete source of protein, has all the nine essential amino acids, trace elements and vitamins needed to survive—hence its recently acquired description as a superfood.

And in case you are wondering what a superfood is, it is food that is packed with lots of powerful antioxidants, vitamins, minerals, essential fatty acids and other nutrients that are not only supposed to keep you healthy, but also may help your body ward off diseases without any side effects or the use of supplements or other chemicals. Superfoods are natural and pure foods that are not packed with preservatives, additives, colors or enhancers. I think quinoa fits in very nicely to this description.

Where does quinoa come from? It is the seed of a leafy plant called Chenopodium Quinoa of the Chenopodium/Goosefoot plant family and is distantly related to the spinach plant. It is perhaps referred to as a grain because it looks like a grain and is about the same size as other grains, whereas a seed can easily imply that it is similar in size as an olive or even an avocado.

Quinoa is an ancient seed native to the Andes Mountains in South America. It has been around for over 5,000 years and is known to have been a staple food of the ancient civilization of the Incas having sustained them for centuries.

It was used to supplement their diet of potatoes and corn. It was commonly referred to as the 'mother grain' or 'gold of the Incas' and was considered sacred.

It is still considered a very important food in the South American kitchen and in the last 10 to15 years has gone from almost total obscurity in the rest of the world, to a much loved, much used, must have, much talked about and publicized superfood that should be in every pantry especially if someone is a vegan, vegetarian, gluten/wheat intolerant or a coeliac.

Quinoa is almost the perfect complete food as the degree of nutrition in each tiny seed is regarded to be quite potent.

It has very high amounts of protein than any other grain and this unusually high amount of protein is actually a complete protein containing all nine essential amino acids. The World Health Authority has found that the quality of the protein in quinoa is the closest to protein found in milk. Quinoa is a must for vegans and vegetarians who may be concerned about the level of protein in their daily diet. It has more calcium than cow's milk, is an excellent antioxidant, is rich in dietary fibre and has more iron than most other grains.

The amino acid composition is also extremely well balanced and has a particularly high content of the amino acid, lysine, which is essential in our diet for tissue repair and growth. It is also a very good source of manganese, magnesium, potassium, phosphorous, copper, zinc, vitamin E, B6, riboflavin, niacin and thiamine. It also has the highest content of unsaturated fats and a lower ratio of carbohydrates than any other "grain" plus it has a low Glycemic Index level.

Needless to say, there are a lot of health benefits to be gained by everyone who adds quinoa to their diet.

Because quinoa is available in seed, flake, flour and puffed forms, it is suitable for cooking in many different ways and lends itself beautifully to so many dishes. The color of the grain can vary from white (opaque), red and black which are the colors available in Australia. It also comes in pale yellow to red, purple and brown and can be sold as tricolor quinoa.

When cooked, it has a very delicate texture making it ideal for soups, sweets, salads, vegetarian and non-vegetarian meals.

It is available at most health food stores and in the health food section of larger supermarkets. Some shops also stock quinoa milk. It is however quite expensive and not that readily available.

What does the quinoa seed look like?

The seed itself is tiny and round with a fine band around it ending in what looks like a minute "tail". As it cooks, the tail spirals out and almost detaches itself becoming very distinct from the rest of the quinoa in the shape of an outer white ring that is clearly visible. When cooked, quinoa becomes very soft in the centre whilst the tail retains a bit of crunch giving it a texture all of its own.

Cooked quinoa has a very delicate texture and it expands to almost four times its original volume. It is very distinctive in appearance and has a lovely slightly nutty taste. It can be substituted for just about any grain, can be used as an accompaniment to a meal (that you would normal serve with rice for example) or it can be used with other ingredients to make a complete meal.

How to prepare quinoa

Quinoa grows in arid climates, at high altitudes and very poor soil. It is suggested that the survival of this plant over the centuries could be attributed to a soapy like substance called "saponin" which creates a bitter coating on the grain and protects it from the high-altitude weather as well as from attack by birds or insects. The recipes in this book use seeds, flakes, flour and puffed quinoa.

Cooking with quinoa seeds

When using quinoa seeds, the bitter soapy coating must be removed before cooking. Although quinoa may be pre-washed and ready to cook when bought, it should still be rinsed thoroughly before use to remove any residue saponin.

Simply place the quinoa seeds into a fine sieve and rinse under cold running water. After thoroughly wetting the quinoa, rub it lightly between your fingertips, drain well and it is ready to cook. Make sure that you do use a very fine sieve as the seeds are so tiny they may go straight through a standard colander or strainer.

Quinoa cooks very quickly simmered in water, stock, juice or milk. One part quinoa, two parts liquid and ten minutes in the saucepan is all that is needed to prepare quinoa as a basic cooked alternative to other grains. However, you may need to cook the quinoa a little longer if the liquid is denser than water, such as a sauce, stock or milk.

Also the red and black varieties take longer than 10 minutes to cook and tend to retain a little bit more of a crunch. A good rule of thumb when cooking the black quinoa is at least 15 minutes and the other thing to look out for is that it should be cooked until you can see quite a bit of the white "tail" circling the seed. The softer it becomes the more you can see the white tail.

The length of the cooking time can also vary depending on the brand and age of the grain. Resting the quinoa in a covered saucepan for 10–15 minutes after cooking will ensure it is softer and fluffier. Use a fork to fluff up the quinoa after it has been cooked and off the heat.

Quinoa can be cooked in the microwave although it is not my preferred method—I find it a bit too fiddly and it seems to take longer. However, to cook quinoa in the microwave, place 1 part quinoa to 2 parts liquid in microwave-proof dish and cook on high for 7 minutes. Stir then cover with plastic wrap and stand for 7–8 minutes. Depending on your microwave you may need to vary the cooking time.

You can also cook quinoa in a rice cooker the same as way as you would on the stove top. One part quinoa to two parts water cooked on the rice setting then rest in the cooker for 5–10 minutes.

For an added nutty taste, you can toast the quinoa before cooking. Rinse and drain the quinoa well then dry roast in a small non-stick frying pan. When the grains start to pop, remove the pan from heat and transfer the quinoa to a saucepan with 2 parts liquid. Bring to the boil, then reduce the heat and simmer, covered, for 10 minutes or so.

To prepare the salads from this book, you will need to cook the quinoa first, cool completely and then combine with the other ingredients. I make a lot salads using quinoa so I tend to cook a large batch of the grain and leave it in the refrigerator to use as I need it.

Quinoa cooked in water will keep in the refrigerator for up to a week and can also be frozen. For most of the other recipes in this book, the quinoa is cooked with the other ingredients—one-pot meals.

Which colored quinoa you wish to use in your cooking is totally up to you. I have specified a color in only a few recipes and that was done purely for visual appeal. Don't forget, the darker colors take an extra 5 minutes or so to cook.

Note: you may read some recipes that suggest roasting quinoa flour before use. I'm not a fan of this for a number of reasons. The quality of the flour has improved a lot recently and some don't have any or very little bitterness. The aftertaste depends on the quality of the brand and the age of the flour. Because I use lots of flavors in my flour, the aftertaste is not usually that noticeable. Also, the roasted flour can very easily burn and, depending on how much you put in the pan and the size of the pan, it can roast very unevenly. I think when chefs roast quinoa flour, they do it in very small batches. But if you want to try roasting the flour, give it a go.

Cooking with quinoa flakes

Quinoa flakes are simply quinoa seeds that have been rolled into very fine flakes. They look like rolled oats only a lot smaller and cook a lot quicker.

The flakes are excellent as a substitute for breadcrumbs and rolled oats and, because quinoa is gluten/wheat free, everyone can enjoy dishes made with them. I would strongly recommend to anyone who is gluten/wheat intolerant to use quinoa flakes as a crumb coating. The Greek Lamb

Cutlets with Minted Yogurt (page 124) are simply delicious. I tend to add lots of herbs and spices to the flakes—it adds a lot more flavor.

Quinoa flakes also make a healthy, delicious breakfast porridge and they are great in smoothies as they thicken the smoothie and provide additional protein. Just 1 to 2 tablespoons added to smoothie gives you that extra protein boost.

You may experience a slightly bitter taste with the flakes because the flakes cannot be rinsed before using, but many people end up loving them.

Cooking with quinoa flour

Quinoa flour is made from quinoa seeds that have been ground. The flour has a slight bitter aftertaste from not being rinsed and needs a little help from raising agents such as baking powder or baking soda (bicarbonate of soda) to add some lightness to whatever you are baking.

Also the bitterness leaves a slight earthy aftertaste which can be masked or enhanced whichever way you want with flavors such as herbs and spices for savory or vanilla, cinnamon and nutmeg for sweet.

You can use the flour to make cakes, pancakes, pasta, pizza bases and as a thickener for sauces. You can even mill your own flour if you have a food processor that allows you to do this.

It is a good idea to store the flour in the freezer until you need it. Just remember take it out about half an hour before you use it.

The distinctly nutty taste is more pronounced in the flour than in the seeds, flakes or puffed quinoa giving it a quite an earthy aroma.

Cooking with puffed quinoa

I have used store-bought puffed quinoa for all the recipes in this book that require puffed quinoa.

Puffed quinoa is the seed that has been popped in a similar way that popcorn comes from corn. Puffed quinoa is very light in weight, has a neutral taste and is quite soft.

It can be used in slices, cakes, as sprinkles or even as toppings to sweet and savory dishes. It makes a good breakfast cereal with milk or sprinkled over other cereals. And it is used widely in the very popular power/energy balls that everyone seems to love.

You will read and hear that you can make your own puffed or popped quinoa. To me this describes quinoa in two different ways—puffed is when it actually looks like a little puff that is very light and airy. Popped is where it is toasted and really looks no different to what the seed looked like originally except that it is darker in color, tastes toasted and is a lot more palatable than having it raw. I have not had much joy puffing quinoa so I prefer the store-bought variety.

Popped or toasted quinoa is very easy to make. You place some quinoa seeds into a heavy-based saucepan over medium heat and leave it on until it starts to pop and brown. Keep an eye on it and keep tossing it regularly. Once it is golden, cool and store it in a glass jar for use in salads or over fruit, cereal and porridge.

Some people like to rinse the quina before popping, but I don't think it is necessary as I find that not washing it adds to the toasted nutty flavor.

For something different: quinoa sprouts

While I have not included any quinoa sprouts in this book, you can sprout quinoa by placing 1 part rinsed quinoa with 3 parts water in a jar with a lid. Soak for about 2 hours, drain and rinse, then return to the jar with the lid on and leave to sprout. You must rinse them at least twice per day. They are very tiny sprouts and should be ready in about 2–3 days but must be eaten immediately as they do not last. Sprouts are lovely in salads.

Cooking times for quinoa seed

All cooking appliances especially ovens are different and vary in their cooking time. You may need to experiment with your own appliances to work out the correct cooking time. On my cook top, I find 10 minutes with a ratio of one part quinoa to two parts water is perfect for the white grain.

However I sometimes find that I need to cook it a little longer if the liquid used is not water and it is dense such as a sauce or milk. I also find that the darker grains can take longer to cook, with the black variety taking even longer than red quinoa. Actual cooking time definitely depends on the color. When cooking the tricolored variety which is a mix of the white, red and black, you will need to cook it for the longer time. While the white quinoa will cook fairly quickly, the darker seeds will need longer. The bonus with tricolor quinoa is that you get different textures in the dish.

When cooking one-pot meals, I find that using a large deep frying pan with a lid is best. It holds quite a bit and distributes and cooks the quinoa more evenly as the heat is spread over a larger cooking surface.

How to find your favorite recipes in this book

The chapters are divided into Seeds, Flakes, Flour and Puffed.

Under these headings, the recipes are grouped under meatless dishes, seafood, chicken, meat, desserts and treats. Not all chapters have all of these groups but we have done this to make it easy for you to find the recipes you know you like.

Conversions from metric to imperial are rounded up or down depending on the conversion. If you use only metric or only imperial, the recipes will work.

Seeds

VEGETARIAN SALADS

Herb and Tomato Salad

Black Bean and Radish Salad

Carrots and Chickpea Salad with Chermoula

Bean Salad

Corn and Herb Salad

Festive Mango and Pomegranate Salad

Pineapple, Ginger and Mint Salad

Pomegranate and Broad Bean Salad

Raw Vegetable Salad

Tomato and Ginger Salad with Salad Sprouts

Super Slaw

Roast Pumpkin and Lentil Salad

Pawpaw and Cucumber Salad with Creamy Coconut Dressing

Herb and Tomato Salad

Ingredients

150 g (5 oz) quinoa, rinsed
and drained
375 ml (12 fl oz) water
1 large red onion, halved
and finely sliced
1 bunch fresh chives,
chopped
½ bunch fresh flat leaf
parsley, chopped
½ bunch fresh dill, chopped
½ bunch fresh basil,
chopped
450 g (18 oz) cherry
tomatoes, halved

Dressing

2 tablespoons red wine
vinegar
3–4 tablespoons extra virgin
olive oil
salt and freshly cracked
black pepper

Serves 6

Method

1. Add quinoa to a medium saucepan with the water. Bring to the boil, reduce heat and cover. Simmer for 10–15 minutes until all the water is absorbed. Remove from heat. Allow to stand for 10–15 minutes. Set aside.
2. Place the cooled quinoa into a bowl and toss with the onion, chives, parsley, dill, basil and tomatoes.
3. Mix all the dressing ingredients together and pour over the salad. Adjust the seasoning and toss together until the salad is well coated with the dressing.
4. Leave to stand for about 30 minutes before serving on a platter.

Note: This salad uses a lot of herbs, you can vary the amount according to your taste and also use any other herb that you like.

Black Bean and Radish Salad

Ingredients

125 g (4 oz) quinoa rinsed
   and drained
330 ml (11 oz) water
1 bunch small radishes
2 x 400 g (14 oz) cans black
   beans, drained and rinsed
350 g (12 oz) fresh green
   beans, cut into pieces and
   blanched
4 scallions (spring onions),
   finely sliced
½ bunch fresh cilantro
   (coriander), chopped

Dressing

1 small clove garlic, very
   finely grated
1 long red chili, deseeded
   and finely chopped
4 tablespoons extra virgin
   olive oil
juice of 1 lime
1 tablespoon white wine
   vinegar
1 tablespoon maple syrup
salt and freshly cracked
   black pepper

Serves 6

Method

1. Place quinoa into a small saucepan with the water. Bring to the boil, reduce the heat, cover and simmer for 10 minutes until all the water is absorbed. Remove from the heat and leave to stand covered for 15 minutes. Cool completely and fluff up with a fork.
2. Slice the radishes into thin rounds—if radishes are big, cut in half then slice. Place in a bowl and add the cooled quinoa, black and green beans, scallions and cilantro. Mix well.
3. Whisk all the dressing ingredients together, taste and adjust the seasoning. Pour over the salad making sure that all ingredients are coated with the dressing.
4. If possible leave to stand for at least an hour before serving. Garnish with extra cilantro leaves.

Carrot and Chickpea Salad
with Chermoula

Ingredients
200 g (7 oz) black quinoa
    rinsed and drained
500 ml (16 fl oz) water
750 g (27 oz) carrots, peeled
    and cut into chunks
2 x 400 g (14 oz) chickpeas,
    drained
cilantro (coriander),
    chopped, to serve
flat leaf parsley, chopped, to
    serve
red chilies, sliced, to serve

Chermoula Paste
4 cloves garlic, chopped
2 tablespoons capers
2–3 anchovy fillets, chopped
1 generous handful fresh
    cilantro (coriander),
    chopped
half a handful fresh flat leaf
    parsley, chopped
1 teaspoon ground sweet or
    smoked paprika
1 generous teaspoon
    ground cumin
½–1 teaspoon chili flakes
juice 1–2 large lemons
125 ml (4 fl oz) extra virgin
    olive oil

Serves 6–8

Method
1. Add quinoa to a medium saucepan with the water. Bring to the boil, reduce heat and cover. Simmer for 10–15 minutes until all the water is absorbed. Remove from heat. Allow to stand for 10–15 minutes then cool completely. Set aside.
2. Blanch the carrots in salted boiling water for about 4–5 minutes only, you want them tender but with a bit of a crunch. Drain and refresh under cold running water.
3. When cooled, place into a bowl with the quinoa and chickpeas.
4. To make the chermoula, place all ingredients into a food processor and process until the chermoula is chopped to the fineness you prefer.
5. Toss in as much of the chermoula paste as you like—I usually use all from the recipe above. Mix well and serve with extra chopped cilantro and parsley sprinkled over and sliced red chilies.

Note: For the chermoula, adjust the amount of ingredients to suit your taste—more of one and less of another. I love lots of anchovies and capers in mine. Any leftover paste will keep for weeks in the refrigerator in a glass jar with a lid.

Bean Salad

— ✤ —

Ingredients

150 g (5 oz) red or tricolor
  quinoa
375 ml (12 fl oz) water
450 g (18 oz) green beans
1 x 400 g (14 oz) tin cannellini
  beans
1 x 400 g (14 oz) tin borlotti
  beans
1 x 400 g (14 oz) tin butter
  beans
1 red onion, halved and
  finely sliced
½ bunch flat leaf parsley,
  finely chopped
4 tablespoons extra virgin
  olive oil
2 tablespoons red wine
  vinegar
salt and freshly cracked
  black pepper

Serves 6–8

Method

1. Place quinoa in a small saucepan with the water. Bring to the boil, reduce heat, cover and simmer for about 15 minutes until all the water is absorbed and the quinoa is tender. Remove from heat and leave to stand covered for 15 minutes then cool completely. Fluff up with a fork.

2. Top and tail and de-string green beans and blanche in boiling salted water for 3 minutes. Drain and place into a bowl filled with cold water and ice cubes to stop the cooking process and also help retain the bright green color of the beans.

3. Drain the beans well again and shake off as much of the excess moisture as possible. Place into a large bowl with the quinoa.

4. Rinse and drain the other beans and add to the bowl with the onion and parsley.

5. Whisk together the olive oil with the vinegar and season to taste.

6. Pour over the beans and mix well to combine. Leave to stand for about 30 minutes before serving.

Corn and Herb Salad

Ingredients

150 g (5 oz) black quinoa,
 rinsed and drained
375 ml (12 fl oz) water
250 g (8 oz) fresh young corn
 spears
500 g (18 oz) corn kernels,
 cooked
4 scallions (spring onions),
 sliced diagonally
1 bunch fresh chives,
 chopped in longish pieces
3 tablespoons flat leaf
 parsley, chopped

Dressing

2 teaspoons Dijon mustard
1 tablespoon runny honey
2 tablespoons white wine
 vinegar
3–4 tablespoons extra virgin
 olive oil
salt and freshly cracked
 black pepper

Serves 6–8

Method

1. Add quinoa to a small saucepan with the water. Bring to the boil and reduce the heat. Cover and simmer for 15–20 minutes until all the water is absorbed. Remove from heat and allow to stand for 15 minutes.
2. Blanche the corn spears in boiling salted water for about 2 minutes. Drain and refresh under cold running water then drain again really well. Leave whole or cut into pieces.
3. Place the cooled quinoa into a bowl with the corn spears, corn kernels, scallions, chives and parsley and mix thoroughly.
4. Mix all dressing ingredients together then pour over the corn and toss to combine. Adjust seasoning to suit your taste. If possible, leave to stand for at least an hour before serving.
5. Serve as a salad for a barbecue or as a side dish with any cold meat or vegetarian dish.

Note: You can substitute the black quinoa with any other color. Keep in mind that black quinoa takes a little longer to cook and will usually always have a little crunch to it.

Festive Mango
and Pomegranate Salad

Ingredients

125 g (4 oz) quinoa, rinsed
   and drained
320 ml (11 fl oz) water
2 mangoes, peeled and cut
   into chunks
2 Lebanese cucumbers, cut
   into chunks
½ red bell pepper (capsicum),
   cut into small chunks
½ yellow bell pepper
   (capsicum), cut into small
   chunks
½ orange bell pepper
   (capsicum), cut into small
   chunks
4 scallions (spring onions),
   sliced
1 handful fresh basil leaves,
   chopped
1 large pomegranate
basil leaves, for garnish

Dressing

juice of 1 lime
1 clove garlic, finely grated
1 tablespoon horseradish
   cream
2–3 tablespoons extra virgin
   olive oil
salt and pepper

Serves 4

Method

1. Add quinoa to a small saucepan with the water. Bring
    to the boil, reduce the heat, cover and simmer for 10
    minutes until all the water is absorbed. Remove from heat.
    Cool completely.
2. Combine quinoa in a bowl with the mangoes, cucumbers,
    capsicums, shallots and basil leaves.
3. Cut the pomegranate in half and, with back of a wooden
    spoon, bash most of the fruit and any juices straight out of
    both halves into the bowl with other ingredients. Reserve
    some of the fruit to use as garnish.
4. Mix all of the dressing ingredients together and pour over
    the salad. Toss well and garnish with extra basil leaves and
    reserved pomegranate seeds.

Note: You can make this salad a meal on its own by
adding cooked chicken or shrimp (prawns)—really
delicious.

Pineapple, Ginger and Mint Salad

Ingredients

100 g (3½ oz) red quinoa,
  rinsed and drained
250 ml (8 oz) water
1 medium fresh pineapple
4 scallions (spring onions),
  finely sliced
1 tablespoon fresh ginger,
  grated
2 long red chilies, deseeded
  (optional) and sliced
handful fresh mint leaves
1 lime, juice and rind
2 tablespoons extra virgin
  olive oil
salt, to taste

Serves 6

Method

1. Add quinoa to a small saucepan with the water and bring to the boil. Reduce heat, cover and simmer on low heat for 10–15 minutes until all the water is absorbed. Set aside to stand for 10–15 minutes then cool completely.
2. Peel and core pineapple and cut into bite-sized pieces.
3. Place the quinoa, pineapple and its juices into a bowl with the scallions, ginger and chilies.
4. Chop some of the mint especially the larger leaves and leave the smaller ones whole. Add the mint to the quinoa/pineapple with the lime juice, rind and olive oil.
5. Toss all the salad ingredients together and season with salt to taste. Cover and refrigerate for at least 1 hour before serving, even longer if possible, to allow all the flavors to combine.
6. Serve with any meat, fish, poultry of vegetarian dish.

Note: This is a very light and fresh tasting salad. It is lovely as a side for barbecued foods.

Pomegranate and Broad Bean Salad

Ingredients

125 g (4 oz) black quinoa, rinsed and drained
330 ml (11 fl oz) water
500 g (18 oz) frozen broad beans
300 g (10 oz) cooked corn kernels
1 bunch fresh chives, chopped
1 large pomegranate

Dressing

1 tablespoon honey
1 tablespoon horseradish cream
3 tablespoons extra virgin olive oil
juice of ½–1 lemon
1 small clove garlic, very finely grated
salt and freshly cracked black pepper

Serves 6–8

Method

1. Place quinoa in a saucepan with the water. Bring to the boil, reduce the heat, cover and simmer for 15 minutes until all the water is absorbed and the quinoa is tender, though black quinoa can have a slight crunch to it. Remove from heat and leave to stand covered for 15 minutes then cool completely.
2. Cook broad beans until tender. When cool enough to handle, remove the outer skin and place beans into a large bowl. Add the corn, cooled quinoa and chives.
3. Cut the pomegranate in half and with the back of a wooden spoon, bash so that the seeds fall out into the bowl. You may need to help some seeds come out. Add pomegranate seeds to other ingredients and mix well.
4. Whisk the dressing ingredients together, pour over the salad and toss to combine.

Note: I like to hold back some of the pomegranate seeds and scatter them over top of salad just before serving.

Raw Vegetable Salad

Ingredients
200 g (7 oz) quinoa, rinsed and
    drained
500 ml (16 fl oz) water

Salad
1 raw beetroot, coarsely grated
2 carrots, coarsely grated
2 courgettes (zucchinis), coarsely
    grated
2 Lebanese cucumbers, coarsely
    grated
1 red onion, coarsely grated
1 baby fennel bulb, coarsely
    grated
3 radishes, coarsely grated
1 small knob ginger, grated
handful mint leaves
1–2 long red or green chilies,
    finely chopped
mint sprigs, for garnish
slices chilli, for garnish

Dressing
165 ml (5½ fl oz) extra virgin olive
    oil
1 clove of garlic, very finely
    grated
3 tablespoons balsamic vinegar
3–4 tablespoon fresh chives,
    finely chopped
salt and pepper

Serves 8–10

Method
1. Place quinoa into a medium saucepan with the water. Bring to the boil, reduce the heat, cover and simmer for 10–15 minutes until all the water is absorbed. Remove from heat and leave to stand covered for 10–15 minutes then cool completely.
2. Place the salad ingredients into a large bowl and gently toss to combine. Toss the quinoa through the salad shortly before serving.
3. To make the dressing, whisk the ingredients together, taste and season with salt and pepper.
4. Transfer salad to a large serving platter, garnish with extra mint leaves and slices of chili. Serve the dressing separately in a jug for everyone to help themselves.

Tomato and Ginger Salad
with Salad Sprouts

Ingredients

125 g (4 oz) quinoa, rinsed
and drained

320 ml (11 fl oz) water

1 knob ginger

250 g (8 oz) grape or cherry
tomatoes, halved

6 scallions (spring onions),
finely sliced

large handful Thai or Italian
basil leaves

250 g (8 oz) salad or alfalfa
sprouts

1–2 long red or green chilies,
deseeded and sliced

Dressing

juice of ½–1 lime

1 small clove garlic, very
finely grated (optional)

1 tablespoon fish sauce

2 tablespoons extra virgin
olive oil or grapeseed oil

Serves 6

Method

1. Add quinoa to a small saucepan with the water. Bring
   to the boil, reduce heat, cover and simmer for 10–15
   minutes until all the water is absorbed. Remove from heat.
   Allow to stand for 10–15 minutes then cool completely.

2. Peel the ginger and using a peeler, shave the ginger into
   thin slices. Use as much or as little ginger as you like.

3. When the quinoa has cooled, place into a bowl with the
   ginger, tomatoes, shallot, basil, sprouts and chilies.

4. Whisk all the dressing ingredients together, pour over the
   salad and gently toss well to combine.

5. Separate the sprouts as you go to ensure that they are
   evenly distributed throughout the salad. Leave to stand
   for at least half an hour for the flavors to develop.

Note: Any of the micro sprouts work well in this recipe.
This salad is also delicious served with peeled cooked
(shrimp) prawns or chopped cooked chicken.

Super Slaw

—+··❈··+—

Ingredients

200 g (7 oz) tri-color quinoa,
  rinsed and drained
500 ml (16 fl oz) water
8 large stalks Cavolo Nero
  (Tuscan) kale
1 tablespoon red wine
  vinegar
¼ small red cabbage,
  trimmed and finely
  shredded
2 medium carrots, coarsely
  grated
2 stalks celery, finely sliced
1 red onion, halved and
  finely sliced
6 scallions (spring onions),
  finely sliced
1–2 long red chilies,
  deseeded and sliced
  (optional)
salt and freshly cracked
  pepper

Dressing

1–2 tablespoons red wine
  vinegar
60–80 ml (2–2½ fl oz) extra
  virgin olive oil
1–2 tablespoons horseradish
  cream

Serves 8–10

Method

1. Place quinoa in a small saucepan with the water, bring to the boil, then reduce the heat, cover and simmer for 10–14 minutes until all the water is absorbed. Remove from heat, stand for 10 minutes, covered then cool completely.
2. Thoroughly wash the kale. Remove and discard most of the lower thick part of the stalk. Place the leaves on top of one another after you have removed the stalk, roll them into a thick cigar shape and finely shred.
3. Place the kale into a bowl and pour in the red wine vinegar. Using your hands rub the vinegar into the kale. This helps to soften and break down the kale.
4. Combine the cooled quinoa with the kale, cabbage, carrots, celery, onion, scallions and chili (if used) in a large bowl.
5. Season with salt and pepper and toss well to combine.
6. Mix together the vinegar, olive oil and horseradish. Pour as little or as much as you like over the salad and mix really well—using your hands is the best way to mix this salad. If possible, cover and chill for 1–2 hours before serving.

Note: This makes a large salad and is great for a crowd. The quinoa adds extra texture and makes it an even healthier. Apart from shredding the kale myself, I tend to prepare the carrots, cabbage, celery and onion in a food processor with the slicing or grating attachment—it is so much easier.

Roast Pumpkin and Lentil Salad

Ingredients

1.5 kg (3 lb 5 oz) butternut
   pumpkin
salt, to season
1–2 tablespoons extra virgin
   olive oil
180 g (6½ oz) quinoa, rinsed
   and drained
375 ml (12 fl oz) water
2 x 400 g (14 oz) tins brown
   lentils, rinsed and drained
1 medium red onion, finely
   sliced
4 scallions (spring onions),
   chopped
125 g (4 oz) fresh cilantro
   (coriander), chopped

Dressing

1 teaspoon cumin seeds
zest and juice of 1 lemon
3–4 tablespoons extra virgin
   olive oil
salt and pepper, to taste

Serves 4–6

Method

1. Pre-heat oven to 190°C (375°F) and line a baking tray with non-stick baking paper.
2. Peel and chop pumpkin into small pieces, season with a little salt and drizzle with extra virgin olive oil. Bake until cooked and charred along the edges (about 20 minutes). Remove from oven and cool.
3. Meanwhile place the quinoa in a small saucepan with the water, bring to the boil, then reduce the heat, cover and simmer for 10 minutes until all the water is absorbed. Remove from the heat and cool completely.
4. Place pumpkin and lentils into a mixing bowl; gently stir in the quinoa, onion, spring onions and coriander.
5. Dry-roast the cumin seeds in a small frying pan until they become fragrant and start to pop. Remove from heat and grind to a fine powder in a mortar and pestle.
6. To make the dressing, mix the cumin together with all the other dressing ingredients, pour over salad and gently toss through.

Pawpaw and Cucumber Salad with Creamy Coconut Dressing

Ingredients

125 g (4 oz) black quinoa, rinsed and drained

375 ml (12 fl oz) water

1 large papaya (pawpaw), red ripe but firm

4 Lebanese cucumbers, diced

1 red onion, finely chopped

1–2 long red chilies, deseeded and sliced

red chilli, sliced, to garnish

Dressing

½–1 lime, zest and juice

3 tablespoons fresh chives, chopped

3 tablespoons fresh cilantro (coriander), chopped

125 ml (4 fl oz) coconut milk

2 teaspoons fish sauce

1 tablespoon maple syrup

½–1 tablespoon extra virgin olive oil

Serves 6

Method

1. Add quinoa to a medium saucepan with the water. Bring to the boil, reduce heat and cover. Simmer for 15–20 minutes until all the water is absorbed. Remove from heat. Allow to stand for 10–15 minutes then cool completely. Set aside.

2. Peel the papaya and cut into bite sized pieces then place into a bowl with the quinoa, cucumbers, onion, and chilies.

3. Whisk all of the dressing ingredients together and pour over the salad.

4. Toss well, taste and adjust the seasoning. Add more dressing as you feel necessary and serve.

Note: If you plan to prepare this salad in advance, it is best to add the papaya and the dressing to the salad about an hour before serving.

VEGETARIAN SOUPS

Watercress Soup
Kale, Quinoa and Roasted Sweet Potato Soup
Creamy Potato, Mushroom and Mustard Soup
Curried Broccoli and Tomato Soup
Spiced Carrot and Leek Soup
Sweet Potato, Pumpkin and Quinoa Soup

Watercress Soup

Ingredients

500 g (18 oz) watercress
2 tablespoons extra virgin olive oil
1 large leek, washed and trimmed
1 large onion, chopped
2 cloves garlic, chopped
1½ tablespoons English mustard
2 L (4 pt) hot chicken or vegetable stock
salt and freshly ground black pepper
90 g (3 oz) quinoa, washed and drained
125 ml (4 fl oz) fresh cream (optional)

Serves 6–8

Method

1. Trim the lower, tougher part of the stalks from the watercress and remove any yellowed leaves. Roughly chop, wash well and set aside.
2. Heat the oil in a large saucepan and sauté the leek and onion on low heat until soft. Add the garlic, cook for about a minute then stir in the mustard.
3. Add the watercress to the pan (reserving some leaves for garnish) with the stock and season to taste keeping in mind that store-bought stock can be salty.
4. When boiling, reduce the heat, cover and simmer for about 15 minutes.
5. Purée the soup in a food processor or blender, return to the pot, increase heat to high and bring back to the boil.
6. Add the quinoa, bring to boil then reduce heat to a simmer and cook for about 20 minutes until quinoa is cooked and soft and the soup has thickened.
7. Serve with a drizzle of fresh cream or alternatively stir the cream through the whole soup.
8. Garnish with a few of the reserved watercress leaves and serve.

Kale, Quinoa and Roasted Sweet Potato Soup

Ingredients

1.5 kg (3 lb 5 oz) sweet
  potato, peeled and cut
  into chunks
2 large red onions, peeled
  and quartered
4–5 cloves garlic, unpeeled
  and left whole
salt and freshly cracked
  black pepper
extra virgin olive oil
4–6 large stalks of kale
8–10 sprigs thyme, chopped
4 L (2 pt) hot chicken or
  vegetable stock
90 g (3 oz) red or black
  quinoa, rinsed and drained
sour cream or Greek yogurt,
  to garnish
fresh chives, to garnish

Serves 6–8

Method

1. Preheat oven to 200°C (400°F) and line a baking tray with non-stick baking paper.
2. Place the sweet potatoes and onions in a single layer on the baking tray with the unpeeled garlic. Season with salt and pepper, drizzle with extra virgin olive oil and give them a good toss.
3. Place in the oven and roast for about 20–25 minutes until tender and slightly charred.
4. Thoroughly wash the kale. Remove and discard the thick lower part of the stalk then chop the leaves very finely. Set aside.
5. When the baked vegetables are ready, remove from oven. Separate the garlic, allow to cool slightly and remove the skin. Place into a large saucepan with the other roasted vegetables and thyme. Pour in the stock, bring to the boil, reduce the heat, cover and simmer for about 10 minutes.
6. Allow to cool slightly then purée in a blender. Return to the saucepan, add the quinoa and bring the soup back up to the boil. Reduce the heat, cover and simmer for 25–30 minutes until the quinoa is almost cooked.
7. Stir in the kale and turn off the heat. Season well with salt and freshly cracked black pepper and leave to stand covered for 10–15 minutes before serving with a good dollop of sour cream or Greek yogurt and fresh chives.

Note: This is quite a thick soup. If you find it too thick, add extra stock or water. For a vegan option, omit the yogurt and serve garnished with a drizzle of extra virgin olive oil.

Creamy Potato, Mushroom and Mustard Soup

Ingredients

1–2 tablespoons olive oil

1 large onion, chopped

2 cloves garlic, chopped

750 g (27 oz) potatoes, peeled and cubed

350 g (12 oz) mushrooms, roughly chopped

1.75 L (3.7) hot chicken or vegetable stock

2 tablespoons grain mustard

salt and freshly cracked black pepper

60 g (2 oz) black quinoa, rinsed and drained

60 ml (2 fl oz) fresh cream (optional)

flat leaf parsley, chopped, to garnish

Serves 6–8

Method

1. Heat oil in a large saucepan. Add the onion and sauté until soft. Stir in the garlic and cook for a few seconds then add the potatoes, mushrooms, stock and mustard.

2. Season with a little salt and pepper to taste. If using store-bought stock, bear in mind that it can be salty.

3. Bring to the boil, reduce the heat and simmer covered on low heat for 20–25 minutes until the potato is tender.

4. Remove the soup from the heat and purée using a stick blender or food processor.

5. Return the soup to the heat, add the quinoa and bring back to the boil.

6. Reduce heat, cover and simmer for about 25–30 minutes stirring occasionally until the quinoa is cooked.

7. Stir in the cream if used and leave the soup to rest for 10 minutes.

8. Serve garnished with a little chopped parsley.

Note: Because the black quinoa was used, this soup has a little bit of a crunch to it. The longer the soup rests, the softer the quinoa becomes. If you prefer a smoother soup, it is best to use the white quinoa. I like to use a stick blender to blend my soups as I find it so convenient. I prefer not to use the cream as I find the soup creamy enough as is.

Curried Broccoli and Tomato Soup

Ingredients

750 g (27 oz) broccoli
1 tablespoon olive oil
1 teaspoon cumin seeds
2 large onions, chopped
2 cloves garlic, chopped
1 tablespoon fresh turmeric, grated
1½ tablespoons curry powder
½ teaspoon dried chili flakes
2 x 400 g (14 oz) tin peeled diced tomatoes, undrained
1.5 L (3 pt) vegetable stock or water
salt and freshly ground black pepper
125 g (4 oz) quinoa, rinsed and drained
500 ml (1 pt) hot water, extra unsweetened Greek yogurt

Serves 8

Method

1. Cut the broccoli into florets. Use as much of the stalks as possible by peeling and roughly chopping. Set aside.
2. Heat oil in a large saucepan, add the cumin seeds and cook for about a minute until they start to change color and become fragrant. Add the onion and sauté until soft and slightly golden. Stir in the garlic and turmeric and cook for about 30 seconds then stir in the curry powder and chili flakes.
3. Add the broccoli, tomatoes and stock to the saucepan. Season with salt and pepper. Bring to the boil, reduce heat and simmer covered on low heat for 20–25 minutes until the broccoli is tender.
4. Remove the soup from the heat and purée using a blender or food processor. Return the soup to the heat, add the extra water, bring back to the boil and stir in the quinoa.
5. Reduce heat, cover and simmer for 25–30 minutes stirring occasionally until the quinoa is cooked.
6. Leave soup to rest for 10–15 minutes before serving with a dollop of yogurt and a good grind of black pepper.

Note: This is a thick soup that makes a large quantity. It is ideal to freeze leftovers for use at a later time. I purée the soups in the pot and there is very little extra washing up to do. Use chicken stock as an alternative if you wish.

Spiced Carrot and Leek Soup

Ingredients

2 tablespoons cilantro (coriander) seeds
2 tablespoons cumin seeds
2 tablespoons extra virgin olive oil
1 large leek, washed and sliced
3 cloves garlic, chopped
1 teaspoon ground sweet or smoked paprika
½–1 teaspoon dried chili flakes
1 tablespoon maple syrup
1 kg (2.2 lb) carrots, peeled and chopped
2 L (4 pt) vegetable stock or water
90 g (3 oz) quinoa, rinsed and drained
juice of 1 lime
handful fresh cilantro (coriander), finely chopped
unsweetened Greek yogurt or sour cream
extra lime juice, to serve

Serves 8

Method

1. Dry roast the cilantro and cumin seeds in a small non-stick frying pan for about 30 seconds until fragrant, making sure they do not burn.
2. Remove from the pan and grind in a mortar and pestle to a fine powder. Set aside.
3. Heat the oil in a large saucepan and sauté the leek and garlic until soft. Stir in the ground spices with the paprika and chili flakes and cook for 1–2 minutes. Add a little extra oil if the pan is too dry.
4. Stir in the maple syrup and carrots. Pour in the stock, bring to the boil, reduce the heat, cover and simmer for about 20–30 minutes until the carrots are tender.
5. Purée the soup and return to the boil. Season with salt and pepper and stir in the quinoa. Reduce heat, cover and simmer for 20–25 minutes until the quinoa is cooked and the soup has thickened.
6. Stir in lime juice and add cilantro. Leave to stand for about 10 minutes.
7. Garnish with a dollop of yogurt or sour cream, extra cilantro and an extra squeeze of lime juice if you like.

Note: Adding sweet or smoked paprika works well in this recipe. It is really up to your own individual taste if you want to add a teaspoon or more of one or the other.

Sweet Potato, Pumpkin and Quinoa Soup

Ingredients
1 tablespoon olive oil
1 large onion, chopped
2–3 cloves garlic, chopped
1 teaspoon ground cumin
½ teaspoon ground
  coriander
750 g (24 oz) sweet potato
750 g (24 oz) butternut
  pumpkin (squash)
2 L (64 fl oz) hot chicken or
  vegetable stock
salt and freshly cracked
  black pepper
90 g (3oz) red quinoa, rinsed
  and drained
light sour cream
lemon juice (optional)

Serves 6

Method
1. Heat the oil in a large saucepan and sauté onion until soft. Add the garlic and cook for about 30 seconds then stir in the cumin and coriander and cook until fragrant.
2. Peel the sweet potato and pumpkin. Roughly cube and add to the saucepan with the stock and season to taste. Bring to the boil, reduce the heat, cover and simmer for 20–30 minutes until the vegetables are tender.
3. Puree soup and bring back to the boil. Add the quinoa, reduce the heat, cover and simmer for 20–25 minutes until the quinoa is cooked and soft. Leave to stand for at least 10–15 minutes before serving. This allows the quinoa to soften more and for the soup to thicken.
4. Serve with a dollop of sour cream and lemon juice if using.

Note: When using red or black quinoa in soups, the cooking time once the quinoa is added is usually longer than if using white quinoa. When cooked in a dense liquid quinoa in general requires longer cooking time than if cooked in water.

VEGETARIAN SIDES AND MAINS

Chickpea and Kale Pilaf with Raisins

Kale, Pumpkin and Chickpea Curry

Mexican Black Beans

Mushrooms with Garlic and Sour Cream

Quinoa Falafel with Tahini Sauce

Savory Peppers and Tomatoes

Roast Pumpkin, Rocket, Cranberry and Pistachio Pilaf

Lentils with Fresh Turmeric and Spinach

Stuffed Aubergines

Spicy Quinoa

Risotto-Style Quinoa with Olives, Tomatoes and Haloumi

Chickpea and Kale Pilaf with Raisins

Ingredients

8 large stalks Cavolo Nero kale
2 tablespoons extra virgin olive oil
1 large onion, chopped
2 cloves garlic, finely chopped
1 teaspoon mustard seeds
2 teaspoons curry powder
1 teaspoon garam masala
2 x 400 g (14 oz) cans chickpeas, drained
1 x 400 g (14 oz) can diced tomatoes, undrained
125 g (4 oz) golden raisins
250 g (9 oz) quinoa, rinsed and drained
500 ml (16 fl oz) vegetable or chicken stock
salt and freshly cracked black pepper
unsweetened Greek yogurt, for serving

Serves 4–6

Method

1. Thoroughly wash the kale. Remove and discard the tough lower part of the stalk and finely shred the leaves.
2. Heat oil in a large frying pan and sauté onion until soft and golden. Stir in the garlic and mustard seeds and cook about 1 minute. Add the curry powder and garam masala and cook for a few seconds until fragrant without burning.
3. Add chickpeas, tomatoes, raisins, quinoa and stock. Season with salt and a good grind of pepper.
4. Bring to the boil, reduce the heat, cover and simmer for 10 minutes.
5. Stir in the kale and cook for another 10 minutes until all the water is absorbed and the quinoa is cooked.
6. Remove from the heat and leave to stand covered for 10 minutes.
7. Serve with a dollop of yogurt.

Kale, Pumpkin and Chickpea Curry

Ingredients

4 large stalks of kale
2 tablespoons olive oil
1 large red onion, halved
   then sliced
4 cloves garlic, chopped
2 long red chilies, deseeded
   and chopped
1 tablespoon fresh ginger,
   grated
1 cinnamon stick
1 tablespoon cumin seeds
2 tablespoons curry powder
   or paste
500 g (18 oz) butternut
   pumpkin (squash), peeled
   and cubed
150 g (5 oz) quinoa, rinsed
   and drained
1 x 400 g (14 oz) tin diced
   tomatoes, undrained
500 ml (16 fl oz) hot
   vegetable stock or water
2 x 400 g (14 oz) tin
   chickpeas, undrained
salt, to taste
handful fresh cilantro
   (coriander)
lime juice, to taste
Greek yogurt, for serving

Serves 4

Method

1. Thoroughly wash the kale. Remove and discard the thick stalks. Chop the leaves and more tender upper part of the stalk and set aside.
2. Heat oil in a large saucepan. Add onion and cook until soft. Add the garlic, chili and ginger and cook for about 30 seconds.
3. Stir in the cinnamon stick, cumin seeds, curry powder and cook for a few seconds until fragrant.
4. Add the pumpkin and stir to completely coat with the other ingredients then stir in the quinoa, tomatoes and stock.
5. Bring to the boil, reduce the heat, cover and simmer on low heat for about 20 minutes until the water is absorbed and the quinoa is tender.
6. Add the kale and chickpeas. Season with salt to taste, cover and simmer on low heat for another 5–10 minutes until quinoa is completely cooked and the kale is tender. Stir in cilantro.
7. Serve with a squeeze of lime juice and a dollop of yogurt.

Note: This is one of our favorite vegetarian family meals and one that we have often.

Mexican Black Beans

Ingredients

300 g (10 oz) quinoa, rinsed
　　and drained
2 large fresh tomatoes,
　　grated
1 red onion, coarsely grated
3 cloves garlic, finely grated
1½–2 teaspoons ground
　　cumin
½–1 teaspoon ground chili
salt and freshly cracked
　　black pepper
625 ml (20 fl oz) vegetable
　　stock
2 x 400 g (14 oz) cans black
　　beans, drained
large handful fresh cilantro
　　(coriander), chopped
juice of 1 lime
sour cream or Greek yogurt,
　　for serving
1 large avocado, peeled and
　　cubed, for serving
dried chili flakes, for serving

Serves 4–6

Method

1. Place quinoa into a saucepan with the tomatoes (with juices), onion, garlic, cumin, chili, salt, pepper and stock. Bring to the boil, reduce the heat and simmer covered for 20 minutes.
2. Stir in the beans and continue cooking for another 10 minutes on low-medium heat until the beans are heated through and all the liquid has evaporated
3. Switch off the heat and stir in the cilantro.
4. Serve with a good squeeze of lime juice, a dollop of sour cream or Greek yogurt, cubes of avocado and more dried chili flakes.

Note: This is really quick to prepare and all in one pan too. You can either have it as a meal on its own or as an accompaniment. To grate a tomato, rub the bottom part of a whole tomato on the coarse part of a box grater. As you grate the skin will separate from the tomato flesh.

Mushrooms with Garlic and Sour Cream

Ingredients

200 g (7 oz) quinoa, rinsed and drained

500 ml (16 fl oz) water

2 tablespoons extra virgin olive oil

1 onion, halved and thinly sliced

750 g (27 oz) mushrooms

3 cloves garlic, finely chopped

salt and freshly ground black pepper

1 bunch garlic chives, cut into pieces

handful flat leaf parsley, coarsely chopped

150 g (5 oz) sour cream (light if you prefer)

extra chives, chopped, to serve

juice of ½–1 lemon, to serve

Serves 4–6

Method

1. Add quinoa to a medium saucepan with the water. Bring to the boil, reduce heat and cover. Simmer for 10–15 minutes until all the water is absorbed. Remove from heat. Allow to stand for 10–15 minutes to cool while you prepare the mushrooms.
2. Wipe mushrooms with a damp cloth to remove any dirt then slice.
3. Heat oil on medium high in a large deep frying pan and sauté the onion until soft.
4. Add the mushrooms and cook until they are tender. Stir in the garlic, season with salt and pepper and cook for 1–2 minutes.
5. Add the quinoa to the mushrooms and gently toss together.
6. Stir in the sour cream and lemon juice and continue cooking on low heat for 2–3 minutes. Add the chives and parsley and cook for another minute or so. Check and adjust seasoning.
7. Garnish with extra chives and a little lemon juice then serve.

Quinoa Falafel with Tahini Sauce

Ingredients

150 g (5 oz) dried broad beans
150 g (5 oz) dried chickpeas
2 teaspoons baking soda
    (bicarbonate of soda)
100g (3 ½ oz) quinoa, rinsed and
    drained
250 ml (8 fl oz) water
6 scallions (spring onions), finely
    chopped
4 cloves garlic, grated
2 teaspoons ground cumin
2 teaspoons ground cilantro
    (coriander)
handful flat leaf parsley, roughly
    chopped
1 small bunch fresh cilantro
    (coriander), roughly chopped
salt and pepper
½–1 teaspoon chili powder
sesame seeds
extra virgin olive oil, for deep frying

Tahini Sauce

180 g (6 oz) tahini paste (sesame
    pulp)
150 ml (5 fl oz) warm water
1 teaspoon brown vinegar
2–3 cloves garlic, finely grated
1½ teaspoon ground cumin
juice of 1–1½ lemons
salt and pepper
3 tablespoons flat leaf parsley, finely
    chopped

Makes about 24

Method

1. Soak the broad beans, chickpeas and 1 teaspoon of baking soda in plenty of cold water for 24 hours.
2. Add quinoa to a medium saucepan with the water. Bring to the boil, reduce heat and cover. Simmer for 10–15 minutes until all the water is absorbed. Remove from heat. Allow to stand for 10–15 minutes then cool completely. Before using, wrap the quinoa in clean tea towel and squeeze out any excess moisture—it needs to be as dry as possible for this recipe.
3. Drain the chickpea and broad beans and remove the skins from the broad beans—they will peel off very easily.
4. Place broad beans, chickpeas, the remaining baking soda, scallions, garlic, cumin, ground coriander, parsley, fresh cilantro, salt, pepper and chili into a food processor and process until you have a fine textured paste that holds its shape when you press it together. Place mixture into a bowl and mix in the quinoa.
5. Shape mixture into round patties. Lightly press some sesame seeds into both sides and fry the falafel in hot oil until golden brown. Drain on paper towels.
6. To make the tahini sauce, place all ingredients into a blender or food processor and process until you have a fluffy smooth paste consistency. Season with salt and pepper to taste.
7. Serve falafel with tahini sauce.

Note: There is really no comparison between homemade falafel and store-bought packet falafel. Although it may sound like hard work, they are very easy to make and the addition of the quinoa make them even healthier. They are ideal for freezing so I usually double or even triple the quantity, freeze in batches (without the herbs) and use as I need adding the herbs to defrosted mix before cooking.

Savory Peppers and Tomatoes

Ingredients

300 g (10 oz) quinoa, rinsed
and drained
750 ml (24 fl oz) hot
vegetable or chicken stock
2 tablespoons extra virgin
olive oil
1 red onion, chopped
2–3 cloves garlic, sliced
1 large green bell pepper
(capsicum)
1 yellow bell pepper
(capsicum)
250 g (8 oz) grape or cherry
tomatoes, washed
salt and pepper
2 tablespoons chives,
chopped
2 tablespoons flat leaf
parsley, chopped

Serves 4–6

Method

1. Place quinoa into a saucepan with the stock. Bring to the boil, reduce heat, cover and simmer for about 10 minutes until all the stock is absorbed. Remove from the heat and leave to stand covered whilst you prepare the remaining ingredients.
2. Heat the oil in a large deep frying pan and sauté the onion until golden and soft. Stir in the garlic and cook until fragrant.
3. Cut the bell peppers into chunks, add to the pan with the tomatoes and cook until the bell peppers start to soften and a little charred and the tomatoes start to blister— don't overcook, you want a little bite left in them.
4. Stir through the quinoa and herbs, season with salt and pepper and cook for 1–2 minutes.
5. Serve as either a side dish or as a vegetarian meal.

Roast Pumpkin, Rocket, Cranberry and Pistachio Pilaf

Ingredients

750 g (27 oz) butternut pumpkin, peeled and cubed

150 g (5 oz) pistachio nuts, shelled

2 tablespoons extra virgin olive oil

2 teaspoons mustard seeds

1 large brown onion, finely chopped

3 cloves garlic, sliced

300 g (10 oz) quinoa, rinsed and drained

625 ml (20 fl oz) hot chicken or vegetable stock

salt and freshly ground black pepper

60 g (2 oz) dried cranberries

125 g (4 oz) fresh rocket

Serves 4

Method

1. Preheat the oven to 200°C (400°F) and line a baking tray with non-stick baking paper.
2. Place the pumpkin on to the tray, drizzle with a little extra virgin olive oil and season with salt and pepper. Roast the pumpkin for about 20 minutes until soft and slightly charred. Set aside.
3. Dry roast pistachio nuts in a small non-stick frying pan until lightly browned. Remove from pan and set aside.
4. Heat oil in a large frying pan and sauté onions until soft and golden. Add the garlic and cook for about 30 seconds.
5. Stir in the quinoa making sure it is well coated in the oil and onion mixture.
6. Pour in the hot stock. Stir well and season with a little salt and pepper. Keep in mind that store-bought stock can be quite salty.
7. Bring to the boil, reduce heat and cover. Simmer for about 15–20 minutes until all the liquid is absorbed and quinoa is cooked.
8. Stir in the rocket and pumpkin and cook until the rocket wilts and the pumpkin is reheated.
9. Transfer to a serving platter and garnish with the cranberries and pistachio nuts.

This can be a vegetarian meal on its own or can be served as a side dish with meat or poultry. My daughters, who are vegetarians, love this dish as it is quick to prepare and delicious.

Lentils with Fresh Turmeric and Spinach

Ingredients

2 tablespoons extra virgin
  olive oil
1 large onion, chopped
2 large cloves garlic, finely
  chopped
1 tablespoon grated fresh
  ginger
1–2 long red chilies,
  deseeded and sliced or
  chopped
2 tablespoons of grated
  fresh turmeric
2 teaspoons ground
  coriander
1 tablespoon ground cumin
2 x 400 g (14 oz) cans lentils,
  undrained
250 g (8 oz) quinoa, rinsed
  and drained
500 ml (16 fl oz) hot
  vegetable stock
salt, to taste
125 g (4 oz) baby spinach
  leaves
large handful fresh cilantro
  (coriander)
1 tablespoon red wine
  vinegar
unsweetened Greek yogurt,
  to serve

Serves 4

Method

1. Heat the oil in a large deep frying pan and sauté onion until soft and lightly browned.
2. Stir in the garlic, ginger, chili and turmeric and cook for about 1 minute. Take the pan off the heat and stir in the ground coriander and cumin, adding a little more oil to the pan if necessary.
3. Return the pan to the heat and cook spices for about 30 seconds until fragrant, stirring constantly so that the spices don't burn.
4. Add the lentils, quinoa and stock. Season with salt. Bring to the boil, reduce the heat, cover and simmer for 15–20 minutes until almost all the liquid is absorbed and the quinoa is cooked.
5. Roughly chop the cilantro leaves and finely chop the stalk and roots and add to the pan with the vinegar.
6. Stir in the spinach and cook only until it wilts. Give the pan a good stir.
7. Remove from heat, cover and leave to stand for about 10 minutes.
8. Serve with a dollop of Greek yogurt.

Note: If you like the taste of vinegar, you may like to add a little more when serving. Lemon juice can be substituted for the vinegar if you prefer.

Stuffed Aubergines

Ingredients

125 g (4 oz) quinoa, rinsed and drained
330 ml (11 fl oz) water
2 x 500 g (18 oz) aubergines (eggplants)
2 tablespoons extra virgin olive oil
extra chives, cut into long pieces, to serve

Filling

2 tablespoons extra virgin olive oil
1 onion, grated
375 g (13 oz) lean minced beef
2 cloves garlic, very finely chopped
1 tablespoon tomato paste
1 x 400 g (14 oz) can diced tomatoes, undrained
½–1 teaspoon ground cinnamon
250 ml (8 fl oz) water
salt and freshly cracked pepper

Topping Sauce

150 g (5 oz) unsweetened Greek Yogurt
2 tablespoons Parmesan cheese, grated
2 tablespoons flat leaf parsley, chopped
salt and pepper

Serves 4

Method

1. Add quinoa to a medium saucepan with the water. Bring to the boil, reduce heat and cover. Simmer for 10–15 minutes until all the water is absorbed. Remove from heat. Set aside to cool.
2. Preheat the oven to 200°C (400°F) and line a baking tray with non-stick baking paper.
3. Cut aubergines in half lengthways and scoop out some of the flesh leaving a solid shell. Brush the inside of the aubergine shells with extra virgin olive oil. Place onto the prepared tray and bake for 25 minutes.
4. Heat the oil in a large non-stick frying and chop the pulp into small pieces. Sauté the aubergine pieces in the oil until golden and soft. Remove from the pan and set aside.
5. To make the filling, heat the oil and sauté the onion until golden. Add the mince and brown all over. Add the garlic and cook for 30 seconds.
6. Stir in the tomato paste, cook for 30 or so seconds then add the aubergine pulp pieces, cinnamon, tomatoes and water. Season with salt and pepper.
7. Bring to the boil, reduce the heat and simmer covered for about 20 minutes. Remove from the heat and mix in the quinoa.
8. Reduce oven temperature to 190°C (375°F). Wipe away any liquid that may have accumulated in the aubergine shells, then pile in the filling.
9. Spoon some of the topping sauce over and bake for about 20 minutes. Remove from heat and allow to cool slightly.
10. Garnish with chives and serve with a salad.

Note: These stuffed aubergines taste very much like the Greek Moussaka without the béchamel sauce.

Spicy Quinoa

Ingredients

300 g (10 oz) quinoa, rinsed
    and drained
750 ml (24 fl oz) hot
    vegetable or chicken stock
2 tablespoons oil
6–8 cardamom pods
1 knob of ginger, sliced
4–5 cloves garlic, sliced
6 scallions (spring onions)
2–3 star anise
handful fresh curry leaves
long dried red chilies, left
    whole (optional)
salt, to taste
handful fresh cilantro
    (coriander), chopped,
    extra for garnish
juice of 1 lime

Serves 4

Method

1. Add quinoa to a medium saucepan with the water. Bring to the boil, reduce heat and cover. Simmer for 10–15 minutes until all the water is absorbed. Remove from heat. Allow to stand for 10–15 minutes. Set aside.
2. Heat the oil in a large frying pan. Lightly crush the cardamom pods and throw them into the pan with the ginger, garlic, scallions, star anise, curry leaves and as many chilies as you like. Stir and cook for about 1–2 minutes until fragrant.
3. Stir in the quinoa, season with salt and continue cooking until the quinoa is heated through. Toss in the cilantro and lots of lime juice.
4. Serve as a side dish with roast meat, seafood or poultry.

Risotto-Style Quinoa with Olives, Tomatoes and Haloumi

Ingredients

1 tablespoon olive oil
1 tablespoon butter
1 large onion, finely chopped
3 cloves garlic, finely grated
60 g (2 oz) sun-dried tomatoes, finely chopped
1 teaspoon dried oregano
1 x 400 g (14 oz) tin diced tomatoes, undrained
200 g (7 oz) quinoa, rinsed and drained
500 ml (16 fl oz) hot vegetable stock
freshly ground black pepper
125 g (4 oz) kalamata olives, pitted and halved
3 tablespoons flat leaf parsley, chopped
extra virgin olive oil, extra
90 g (3 oz) haloumi cheese, coarsely grated
60 g (2 oz) Parmesan cheese, grated
flat leaf parsley, roughly chopped, to garnish

Serves 4

Method

1. Add oil and butter to a large saucepan on medium heat until the butter melts. Add the onion and sauté until soft. Stir in the garlic, sun-dried tomatoes and oregano and cook for about 1 minute.
2. Add the tomatoes, quinoa and stock. Season with pepper to taste—no need to season with salt as there are ingredients in this dish that are quite salty including the olives and cheese.
3. Stir well. Bring to the boil, reduce the heat, cover and simmer for about 20 minutes until all the stock is almost absorbed. If you think of it—and only if you think of it— give the pot a stir once or twice.
4. Stir in the olives and cook for another 5 minutes then stir in the parsley, a good drizzle of olive oil, haloumi and Parmesan cheese.
5. Remove from the heat and leave to stand for about 5 minutes until the quinoa is soft and creamy.
6. Serve with parsley and a little more Parmesan sprinkled over.

Note: This is one of my favorite ways to have quinoa. It is simply delicious and, unlike with risotto, the stock is added at once and you don't have to stir constantly.

SEAFOOD

Fennel, Smoked Salmon and Avocado Salad
Shrimp, Avocado and Herb Salad

Fennel, Smoked Salmon and Avocado Salad

Ingredients

100 g (3½ oz) tricolor quinoa, rinsed and drained
250 ml (8 fl oz) water
2 baby fennel bulbs
2 large avocadoes, peeled and cubed
250 g (9 oz) grape or cherry tomatoes
1 red onion, finely chopped
1–2 tablespoons baby capers
3–4 tablespoons fresh dill, chopped
300 g (10 oz) smoked salmon
fennel fronds, to garnish

Dressing

60 ml (2 fl oz) extra virgin olive oil
2 tablespoons lemon juice
2 teaspoons Dijon mustard
1 tablespoon honey
1 small clove garlic, very finely grated
salt, to taste

Serves 6–8

Method

1. Add quinoa to a medium saucepan with the water. Bring to the boil, reduce heat. Cover and simmer for 10–15 minutes until all the water is absorbed. Remove from heat and allow to stand for 10–15 minutes then cool completely. Set aside.
2. Cut the fennel in half and finely slice. Reserve any of the fronds to use as garnish later. Place fennel into a large bowl with the quinoa, avocadoes, tomatoes, onion, capers and dill.
3. To make the dressing, whisk all the ingredients together. Pour over the salad and gently toss to combine. Transfer salad onto a large serving platter and drape the smoked salmon slices through and on top of the salad.
4. Garnish with the fennel fronds or extra dill and capers.

Note: This salad is lovely for a special occasion or as an entrée when you have guests. It looks stunning on a lovely serving platter.

Shrimp, Avocado and Herb Salad

Ingredients

125 g (4 oz) tricolor quinoa,
    rinsed and drained
320 ml (11 fl oz) water
500 g (18 oz) cooked shrimp
    (prawns),deveined and
    tails left intact
2 Lebanese cucumbers, cut
    into small pieces
4 tablespoons flat leaf
    parsley, finely chopped
2 tablespoons fresh mint,
    chopped
1 bunch fresh chives,
    chopped
1–2 long red chilies,
    deseeded and chopped
2 large avocadoes
lettuce or baby rocket
    leaves, to serve
mint sprigs, to serve

Dressing

4 tablespoons extra virgin
    olive oil
½ lime, juice and zest
salt, to taste

Serves 4–8

Method

1. Place quinoa in a small saucepan with the water. Bring to the boil, reduce heat, cover and simmer for 15 minutes until all the water is absorbed. Remove from the heat and leave to stand covered until cool. Fluff up with a fork.
2. Cut the avocadoes in half then take a very thin small slice off the bottom of each half for balance on the serving plate. Carefully scoop out most of the flesh leaving a firm shell. Finely chop the scooped out flesh.
3. Place the shrimp into a large bowl with the cooled quinoa, cucumber, parsley, mint, chives, chili and avocado flesh and gently toss to combine.
4. Whisk together the oil with the lime juice and zest and season with salt. Adjust using extra lime or salt to suit your taste.
5. Pour the dressing over salad mix, toss well and allow flavors to combine for at least one hour before serving.
6. Pile the salad into the avocado halves and serve as an entrée or main on a bed of lettuce or baby rocket leaves. Garnish with mint sprigs.

Note: Shrimp can be substituted with cooked chicken. For a vegetarian option, leave out the shrimp and add another vegetable or small grape tomatoes.

MEAT SOUPS, SIDES AND MAINS

Beef, Bacon and Kale Soup

Spicy Lamb Shank Soup

Mushrooms with Pork and Ginger

Bacon, Potato and Quinoa Rösti

Mushrooms and Bacon with Maple Syrup

Chorizo Sausage, Kale and Olive Frittata

Bacon, Sun-Dried Tomato, Olive and Feta Savory Cakes

Beef, Olive and Tomato Slice

Plum Pork with Cilantro and Chili Quinoa

San Choy Bow on a Plate

Turkey and Bacon Loaf

Beef with Peas, Tomatoes and Minted Quinoa

Baked Quinoa with Pancetta, Corn and Spinach

Italian Sauasage and Sweet Potato Loaf

Chicken, Chili and Curry Leaf Pilaf

Nasi Goreng

Chicken and Spinach au Gratin

Shrimp and Chorizo Sausage with Caramelized Lemons

Beef, Bacon and Kale Soup

Ingredients

4 stalks Cavolo Nero kale

1–2 tablespoon extra virgin olive oil

600 g (1 lb 3 oz) chuck steak, cut into small thin strips

4 rashers streaky bacon, chopped

1 leek, finely sliced

1 onion, finely chopped

3 cloves garlic, finely chopped

1 x 400 g (14 oz) tin diced tomatoes

2 L (4 pt) beef stock

2 tablespoons Worcestershire sauce

100 g (3½ oz) quinoa, rinsed and drained

Parmesan cheese, grated

Serves 6

Method

1. Thoroughly wash the kale. Remove and discard the stalk and finely shred the leaves. Set aside.
2. Heat the oil in a large heavy-based saucepan and brown the meat all over. Add the bacon, leak, onion and garlic and cook until the leek and onion are soft.
3. Stir in the tomatoes, stock, Worcestershire sauce and season with salt and pepper.
4. Bring to the boil, reduce heat and simmer for 20 minutes until meat is quite tender.
5. Stir in the quinoa and continue cooking on low heat for another 20 minutes. Add the kale and cook for a further 5 minutes.
6. Take off the heat and leave to stand, covered for about 10 minutes.
7. Serve with freshly grated Parmesan cheese.

Spicy Lamb Shank Soup

Ingredients

1–2 tablespoons extra virgin
   olive oil
2 large lamb shanks
1 large onion, finely
   chopped
2 carrots, finely chopped
2 sticks celery, finely
   chopped
2 cloves garlic, finely grated
2–3 tablespoons harissa
   paste, to taste
1 x 400 g (14 oz) tin diced
   tomatoes, undrained
2 L (4 pt) chicken or
   vegetable stock
125 g (4 oz) quinoa, rinsed
   and drained
salt and pepper
juice of ½–1 lemon or lime
flat leaf parsley, chopped, for
   garnish

Serves 6

Method

1. Heat oil in a large saucepan and brown the shanks all over then remove from the pan and set aside.
2. Add the onion, carrot and celery to the pan and cook until soft. Stir in the garlic and cook for about 30 seconds then stir in harissa paste and cook for about 1 minute.
3. Add the tomatoes and return the shanks to the pot with the stock. Bring to the boil, reduce the heat, cover and simmer for about 1½ hours or until the shanks are cooked and start to fall off the bone. Remove the shanks from the pot and keep warm.
4. Add the quinoa to the soup, bring back to the boil, reduce the heat, cover and simmer for about 20–25 minutes until the quinoa is cooked.
5. Finely shred the meat from the shank, return to the soup and season with salt and pepper. Stir well and simmer for another 5–8 minutes until the lamb is heated through. Stir through the lemon or lime juice.
6. Serve with a good sprinkle of parsley.

Note: This soup is delicious on a cold winter's day or night. And it's a dish you can prepare in advance—and it tastes even better if prepared one or two days before z re-heating and serving.

   Harissa paste is a Middle Eastern chili paste and available at most delicatessens and supermarkets.

Mushrooms with Pork and Ginger

Ingredients

100 g (3½ oz) quinoa, rinsed
   and drained
250 ml (8 fl oz) water
300 g (10½ oz) minced pork
3 scallions (spring onions),
   finely sliced
1 generous tablespoon fresh
   ginger, grated
2 cloves garlic, grated
1 long red chili, deseeded
   and chopped
½ teaspoon sesame oil
1 tablespoon soy sauce
1 extra large egg
6 large mushrooms
sesame seeds
scallions (spring onions),
   finely sliced, to serve
soy sauce, to serve

Serves 6

Method

1. Add quinoa to a medium saucepan with the water. Bring to the boil, reduce heat and cover. Simmer for 10–15 minutes until all the water is absorbed. Remove from heat. Allow to stand for 10–15 minutes then set aside to cool.
2. Preheat the oven to 200°C (400°F) and line a baking tray with non-stick baking paper.
3. Place the pork in a bowl with the scallions, ginger, garlic, chili, sesame oil, soy sauce, egg and quinoa and mix well to thoroughly combine.
4. Wipe over the mushrooms with a cloth to remove any dirt and remove the stalk. Fill each with the pork mixture and place on the baking tray.
5. Sprinkle the mushrooms with sesame seeds and a drizzle with oil. Bake for about 20–30 minutes until the pork is cooked and golden.
6. Garnish with sliced scallions, a drizzle of soy sauce and serve with a green salad.

Bacon, Potato and Quinoa Rösti

Ingredients

125 g (4 oz) white quinoa, rinsed and drained
330 ml (11 fl oz) water
125 g (4 oz) streaky bacon, chopped into small pieces
750 g (27 oz) potatoes, peeled and coarsely grated
1 onion, coarsely grated
2 cloves garlic, finely grated
1 bunch chives, finely chopped
1–2 tablespoons flat leaf parsley, finely chopped
1 tablespoon fresh thyme leaves
3 extra large eggs
salt and freshly cracked black pepper

Serves 6–8

Method

1. Add quinoa to a small saucepan with the water. Bring to the boil, reduce heat, cover and simmer for 10minutes until all the water is absorbed. Remove from heat, cover and leave to stand for 10 minutes. Set aside to cool completely.
2. Cook the bacon in a small non-stick frying pan until golden. Drain and set aside.
3. Squeeze as much moisture out of the potatoes as you can then tightly wrap in a clean tea towel with the onions and continue squeezing until the potatoes and onions are fairly dry.
4. Preheat oven to 200°C (400°F) fan forced. Grease a large baking dish, approximately 38 x 26 x 5 cm (15 x 10 x 2 inch), with extra virgin olive oil.
5. Place the potatoes and onion into a bowl with the quinoa, bacon, garlic, chives, parsley, thyme leaves and eggs and mix well to combine. Season with salt and pepper.
6. Spread the mixture into the prepared dish. Drizzle over with a little olive oil and bake for about 30–40 minutes until golden. Remove from oven and allow to stand for about 10 minutes before cutting and serving.

Note: Substitute bacon with ham or leave out altogether for a vegetarian option. Leftovers can be kept in the refrigerator for a couple of days (if it lasts that long). It is delicious eaten at room temperature—no need to reheat.

Mushrooms and Bacon with Maple Syrup

Ingredients

150 g (5 oz) quinoa, rinsed
and drained
375 ml (12 fl oz) water
2 tablespoons extra virgin
olive oil
300 g (10 oz) streaky bacon,
sliced
125 ml (4 fl oz) maple syrup
500 g (18 oz) mushrooms,
sliced
6 scallions (spring onions),
sliced
3–4 cloves garlic, sliced
2 tablespoons flat leaf
parsley, chopped
salt and freshly cracked
black pepper

Serves 4

Method

1. Add quinoa to a medium saucepan with the water. Bring to the boil, reduce heat. cover and simmer for 10–15 minutes until all the water is absorbed. Remove from heat. Allow to stand for 10–15 minutes. Set aside to cool.
2. Heat oil in a large deep frying pan and cook bacon on medium-high heat until just lightly golden.
3. Reduce the heat and pour in some of the maple syrup and continue to cook until the bacon becomes caramelized but not too crispy or burnt. Remove the bacon from the heat and set aside.
4. Add a little more oil to the pan if necessary, add the mushrooms and continue cooking on medium-high heat until they collapse and are golden and cooked.
5. Stir in the scallions and garlic and continue cooking for 1–2 minutes. Add the remaining maple syrup and continue cooking for another 2–3 minutes until the mushrooms have caramelized.
6. Stir in the quinoa and the bacon with the parsley and season with salt and pepper to taste.
7. Toss everything together so as to coat well and serve.

Note: This is delicious meal on its own or as a side dish. For a vegetarian option, leave out the bacon and use cooked tofu instead. Lovely for breakfast with a cooked egg on top, either poached or fried.

Chorizo Sausage, Kale and Olive Frittata

Ingredients

90 g (3 oz) quinoa, rinsed
and drained
250 g (8 fl oz) water
4 stalks kale
1 tablespoon olive oil
2 chorizo sausages, sliced
1 red onion, halved and
sliced
2 cloves garlic, finely
chopped
150 g (5 oz) roasted red bell
pepper (capsicum), cut
into strips
10–12 Kalamata olives,
pitted and halved
8 extra large eggs
salt and freshly cracked
pepper
90 g (3 oz) feta cheese,
coarsely grated
fresh rocket leaves, to
garnish

Serves 6

Method

1. Add quinoa to a medium saucepan with the water. Bring to the boil, reduce heat and cover. Simmer for 10–15 minutes until all the water is absorbed. Remove from heat. Allow to stand for 10–15 minutes. Set aside to cool.
2. Thoroughly wash the kale. Remove the stalks and finely chop the leaves and set aside.
3. Heat oil in a medium sized non-stick frying pan. Add the chorizo and cook for 2–3 minutes until it starts to change color. Remove from the pan with a slotted spoon and set aside.
4. Add the onion and garlic to the pan adding a little extra oil if necessary and cook until the onion is soft.
5. Stir in the kale and cook for 3–4 minutes until it wilts. Return the chorizo to the pan and add the bell pepper, quinoa, olives and mix to combine.
6. Meanwhile heat your grill to medium.
7. Whisk the eggs and season to taste with a little salt if necessary and a good grind of pepper. Add the feta and stir into the eggs.
8. Pour the eggs into the pan and give the pan a good swirl making sure that all the ingredients are mixed into the eggs.
9. Reduce heat to low and cook until the eggs have set at the bottom but are still a little runny on the top.
10. Place the pan under the preheated grill for 3–5 minutes until the top of the frittata is set and lightly browned.
11. Leave to rest for 5 minutes, and then slide the frittata onto a serving plate.
12. Cut into wedges or pieces and serve either warm or cold with some fresh rocket leaves.

Bacon, Sun-Dried Tomato, Olive and Feta Savory Cakes

Ingredients

100 g (3½ oz) tricolor quinoa, rinsed and drained

250 ml (8 fl oz) water

125 g (4 oz) bacon, finely chopped

125 g (4 oz) sun-dried tomatoes, drained and finely chopped

4 scallions (spring onions), thinly sliced

2 clove garlic, finely grated/chopped

3 extra large eggs, lightly beaten

90 g (3 oz) feta cheese

freshly ground black pepper

Makes 6 cakes

Method

1. Add quinoa to a small saucepan with the water. Bring to the boil, reduce heat and cover. Simmer for 10–15 minutes or until all the water is absorbed. Leave to stand and cool slightly.
2. Preheat the oven to 200°C (400°F) and grease a 6-cup non-stick muffin tin.
3. Brown the bacon in a non-stick frying pan without any oil as the bacon will render its own fat until crispy.
4. Remove from the pan and add to a large bowl with the quinoa, tomatoes, scallions and garlic. Mix well then stir in the eggs and mix well until all the ingredients have combined.
5. Crumble in the feta cheese and gently fold through. Season with a good grind of pepper and a little salt if necessary—feta is often very salty. Spoon into the prepared muffin tin.
6. Bake for about 25–30 minutes or until the skewer comes out clean when tested.
7. Leave to cool slightly in tins for about 5 minutes before lifting out onto a wire rack to cool.
8. Serve with a crisp green salad.

Note: Whenever I make these, I like to make a little outer cases for them from non-stick baking paper. I cut a piece long and wide enough to cover each cup of the muffin tin then I fold the paper into place. Apart from liking the look of it when the cakes are served, it makes sure that the cakes do not stick to the tin.

Beef, Olive and Tomato Slice

Ingredients

200 g (7 oz) quinoa grain, rinsed and drained
500 ml (16 fl oz) water
2 tablespoons olive oil
1 large onion, finely chopped
500 g (18 oz) ground beef
2–3 cloves garlic, finely chopped
1 teaspoon cumin seeds
1 heaped tablespoon ground cumin
1 tablespoon soy sauce
180 g (6 oz) frozen peas
125 ml (4 fl oz) water
6 eggs, lightly beaten
handful Kalamata black olives, pitted and halved
3–4 tablespoons Parmesan cheese, grated
salt and pepper
250 g (8 oz) grape or cherry tomatoes
salad, to serve
sweet chili sauce, to serve

Serves 6–8

Method

1. Add quinoa to a medium saucepan with the water. Bring to the boil, reduce heat and cover. Simmer for 10–15 minutes until all the water is absorbed. Remove from heat. Allow to stand for 10–15 minutes. Set aside.
2. Preheat the oven to 200°C (400°F) and lightly grease a 38 x 26 x 5 cm (15 x 10 x 2 in) ovenproof dish.
3. Heat oil in a large deep frying pan. Add the onions and cook until soft and golden. Add the mince and continue to cook until all meat has browned.
4. Stir in the garlic, cumin seeds and ground cumin. Cook for a further 1–2 minutes.
5. Add the soy sauce, peas and water. Season with salt and pepper to taste and cook uncovered on medium heat for about 5 minutes. Cool slightly.
6. Transfer to a bowl and mix in the quinoa, egg mixture, olives and cheese.
7. Adjust seasoning then pour mixture into the greased baking dish. Arrange tomatoes on top and drizzle with a little extra virgin olive oil.
8. Bake for about 25–30 minutes, or until cooked.
9. Serve with a fresh salad and sweet chili sauce.

Plum Pork with Cilantro and Chili Quinoa

Ingredients
750 g (27 oz) pork fillets

Marinade
150 g (5 oz) plum sauce
¼ teaspoon five spice
  powder
1 tablespoon light soy sauce
½–1 teaspoon dried chili
  flakes
1 teaspoon oil
2 cloves garlic, grated

Cilantro and Chili Quinoa
300 g (10 oz) quinoa, rinsed
  and drained
750 ml (24 fl oz) water
1 tablespoon oil
2–3 cloves garlic, sliced
6 scallions (spring onions),
  sliced
2 long red chilies, sliced,
  extra, for garnish
3 star anise
1 small bunch cilantro
  (coriander) leaves, extra,
  for garnish
lime juice, to taste
salt, optional

Serves 4

Method
1. To prepare the pork for the marinade, prick a few times with a fork to allow the marinade to penetrate the meat.
2. Combine all the marinade ingredients. Coat the pork fillets with marinade, cover and put in the refrigerator for about 1–2 hours.
3. Place quinoa into a saucepan with the water. Bring to the boil, reduce the heat, cover and simmer for about 10 minutes until all the water is absorbed. Set aside.
4. Preheat the oven to 200°C (400°F).
5. Remove pork from refrigerator and allow to stand at room temperature for 5–10 minutes.
6. Roast the pork for about 20–25 minutes until cooked to your liking then remove from the oven, loosely cover with foil and rest for about 10 minutes before slicing.
7. While the pork is resting, heat the oil in a deep frying pan and gently sauté the garlic, scallions and chilies until soft. Add star anise then stir in the quinoa, cilantro and lime juice. Mix to combine all the ingredients and season with salt if necessary.
8. Cook any leftover marinade in a small saucepan with a little bit of water for about 5 minutes until thick.
9. Slice the pork and glaze with the cooked marinade and any marinade from the baking dish. Serve on a bed of the cilantro and chili quinoa and garnish with extra cilantro leaves and slices of chili.

San Choy Bow on a Plate

Ingredients

250 g (9 oz) quinoa, rinsed and
  drained
625 ml (20 fl oz) water
2 tablespoons extra virgin
  olive oil
500 g (18 oz) pork mince
6 scallions (spring onions),
  finely chopped
4 cloves garlic, grated
1 tablespoon fresh ginger,
  grated
2 long red chilies, sliced
150 g (5 oz) water chestnuts
  (canned), drained and sliced
150 g (5 oz) fresh beans, sliced
1 red bell pepper (capsicum),
  finely chopped
1 carrot, finely chopped
1 teaspoon palm sugar
4 tablespoons fish sauce
2 tablespoons soy sauce
½ teaspoon sesame oil
1 bunch fresh cilantro
  (coriander) leaves, roughly
  chopped, extra to serve
150 g (5 oz) bean sprouts,
  extra to serve
juice of 1–2 limes
1 red chili, sliced, to serve

Serves 6

Method

1. Add quinoa to a medium saucepan with the water. Bring to the boil, reduce heat and cover. Simmer for 10–15 minutes until all the water is absorbed. Remove from heat. Allow to stand for 10–15 minutes then cool completely. Set aside.
2. Heat oil in a wok or a large frying pan. Add mince and sauté until it is sealed all over breaking up any lumps as it cooks.
3. Add scallions, garlic, ginger and chilies. Stir constantly and cook for about one minute until fragrant.
4. Add the water chestnuts, beans, bell peppers and carrot and stir well. Stir in the sugar, fish and soy sauces, sesame oil and water. Cook for about 3–5 minutes until all the vegetables are just tender.
5. When cooked, stir through the quinoa, cilantro, bean sprouts and as much lime juice as you like.
6. Serve with extra bean sprouts, cilantro and slices of chili.

Note: Traditionally San Choy Bow is served in crisp lettuce cups. Because this dish has the quinoa stirred through, you really don't need the lettuce. My family prefer it served this way but serve with iceberg lettuce leaves if you wish.

Turkey and Bacon Loaf

Ingredients

125 g (4 oz) tricolor quinoa, rinsed and drained

320 ml (11 fl oz) water

3 stalks kale

1 kg (36 oz) turkey mince

125 g (4 oz) bacon, chopped into small pieces

1 large onion, finely chopped

2 cloves garlic, finely grated

1 teaspoon dried thyme

1 teaspoon dried oregano leaves

3 tablespoons fruit chutney of choice

2 extra large eggs, lightly beaten

salt and freshly ground black pepper

fruit chutney or ketchup, to serve

rocket leaves, to garnish

truss tomatoes, to garnish

Serves 6–8

Method

1. Add quinoa to a small saucepan with the water. Bring to the boil, then reduce heat. Cover and simmer for 10–15 minutes until all the water is absorbed. Remove from the heat and set aside covered to cool completely.

2. While the quinoa is cooking, thoroughly wash the kale. Remove the stalk and discard. Chop the leaves very finely and set aside.

3. Preheat the oven to 200°C (400°F) and lightly grease a non-stick medium loaf tin, approximately 20–25 cm (7½–10 inch) with a little olive oil.

4. Add turkey mince to a bowl with the bacon, onion, garlic, thyme, oregano and chutney and mix. Add in the cooled quinoa, kale and eggs and mix very well to combine all the ingredients.

5. Place turkey mixture into the prepared tin and bake for about 1 hour until golden. Remove from the oven and allow to stand for 10 minutes before turning out.

6. Serve with your favorite fruit chutney or ketchup. Garnish with rocket leaves and small truss tomatoes.

Note: Refrigerate leftovers. This loaf is delicious served at room temperature and leftovers make great sandwiches.

Beef with Peas, Tomatoes and Minted Quinoa

Ingredients
3 tablespoons extra virgin
   olive oil
750 g (27 oz) beef, cubed
1 large onion, chopped
3 cloves garlic, chopped
3 tablespoons tomato paste
   (purée)
½–1 teaspoon sugar
2 x 400 g (14 oz) can diced
   tomatoes, undrained
250 ml (4 fl oz) hot water
salt and freshly cracked
   pepper
500 g (18 oz) frozen peas

Minted Quinoa
300 g (10 oz) quinoa, rinsed
   and drained
750 ml (24 fl oz) water
1 mint sprig
1 tablespoon extra virgin
   olive oil
3 tablespoons fresh
   chopped mint
salt and pepper

Serves 4

Method
1. Heat the oil in a large saucepan. Add the meat and cook until browned. Remove from the pan and set aside.
2. Add the onion to the pan and cook until onion is soft. Stir in the garlic and cook for another 30 seconds.
3. Add the tomato paste and sugar and cook for 1–2 minutes stirring regularly until you see the tomato paste start to caramelize without burning.
4. Return the meat to the pan. Stir in the tomatoes and water. Season with salt and pepper. Bring to the boil, reduce the heat, cover and simmer for about 1–1¼ hours or until the meat is tender. Add a little more water if you find the sauce is drying out.
5. Add the frozen peas, bring back up to the boil and continue to cook on a simmer for about 5–7 minutes until the peas are cooked.
6. In the meantime, cook the quinoa in a medium saucepan with the water and a sprig of mint. Bring to the boil, reduce the heat and simmer for 10–15 minutes, or until all the water is absorbed. Remove from heat, remove the sprig of mint and leave to rest covered for 5–10 minutes.
7. Heat the oil in a large frying pan, add the chopped mint and cook for a few seconds to release its fragrance. Stir in the quinoa and season with salt and pepper. Use more mint if you like.
8. Serve the minted quinoa with the beef and peas.

Note: This is a dish that my mother used to cook a lot when I was a child and I, in turn, cooked it for my children. As a kid, it was always served with rice but I now make the meat or non-meat version with the minted quinoa.

Baked Quinoa with Pancetta, Corn and Spinach

Ingredients

1–2 tablespoons extra virgin olive oil
150 g (5 oz) pancetta, diced
1 medium onion, finely chopped
4 scallions (spring onions), sliced
2–3 large cloves garlic, finely chopped
2 tablespoons tomato paste
250 g (9 oz) quinoa, rinsed and drained
salt and freshly cracked black pepper
575 ml (1 pt 2 fl oz) hot chicken stock
250 g (9 oz) frozen corn
125 g (4 oz) baby spinach leaves
knob of butter
3 tablespoons Parmesan cheese, grated
Parmesan cheese, shaved, for serving
lemon juice (optional)

Serves 4

Method

1. Preheat the oven to 200°C (400°F).
2. Heat the oil in a large deep ovenproof frying pan with a lid. Add the pancetta and cook until crisp. Remove from the pan with a slotted spoon and set aside.
3. Add onion and scallions to the pan and cook on medium-high heat until soft and golden. Stir in the garlic and cook for another 30 seconds or so until fragrant.
4. Stir in the tomato paste and quinoa and season with a little salt and pepper—keep in mind that store-bought stock may be salty.
5. Pour in the stock, give it a good stir. Cover and bake in the oven for 20 minutes.
6. Add the frozen corn, stir well and bake for a further 5–7 minutes.
7. Remove from the oven, add the spinach and butter and stir until the spinach wilts.
8. Stir in the pancetta and Parmesan and leave to stand for 2–3 minutes.
9. Serve garnished with shavings of Parmesan cheese and a squeeze of lemon juice.

Note: This is such an easy baked (risotto-style) quinoa to make as you don't have to stand over the stove for 30 minutes stirring and adding the stock a little at a time. It is also just as delicious without the pancetta for a vegetarian option.

Italian Sausage and Sweet Potato Loaf

Ingredients

150 g (5 oz) quinoa, rinsed
   and drained
750 ml (24 fl oz) water
600 g (21 oz) Italian
   sausages, skin removed
500 g (18 oz) orange sweet
   potato, peeled and
   coarsely grated.
250 g (9 oz) courgette
   (zucchini), coarsely grated
2–3 cloves garlic, finely
   grated
4 scallions (spring onions),
   thinly sliced
1 tablespoon English
   mustard
2 tablespoons finely
   chopped fresh parsley
1 teaspoon dried fennel
   leaves
1 teaspoon fresh thyme,
   finely chopped
2 eggs, lightly beaten
salt and freshly ground
   pepper

Serves 6

Method

1. Add quinoa to a medium saucepan with the water. Bring to the boil, reduce heat and cover. Simmer for 10–15 minutes until all the water is absorbed. Remove from heat. Allow to stand covered for 10–15 minutes. Set aside to cool.

2. Preheat oven to 200°C (400°F). Lightly oil a 26 x 14 x 8 cm (10 x 5½ x 3 inch) loaf tin and line the bottom with non-stick baking paper. Make sure the paper comes all the way up the 2 longer sides of the tin. This allows for easy removal of the loaf once cooked.

3. Break up the meat from inside the sausages so that there are no lumps and place in a bowl with the quinoa, sweet potato, courgette, garlic, scallions, mustard and herbs and mix really well until thoroughly combined.

4. Mix in the eggs and season with salt and pepper. Place into the prepared loaf tin and bake for about 1–1¼ hours or until cooked and golden.

5. Leave to rest in the tin for 10–15 minutes before lifting out.

6. Slice and serve with a tomato salad or other salad of choice.

Note: This sausage loaf can be also eaten cold and it makes a delicious sandwich filling. It is ideal to take on picnics or to take to work with a salad.

Chicken, Chili and Curry Leaf Pilaf

Ingredients

400 g (14 oz) quinoa, rinsed
and drained

1 L (2 pt) water

8 chicken tenderloins,
trimmed

1 teaspoon extra virgin olive
oil

1 teaspoon sweet paprika

2–3 tablespoons extra virgin
olive oil

1 tablespoon black mustard
seeds

1 tablespoon yellow mustard
seeds

1 teaspoon nigella seeds
(onion seeds)

50 g (5 oz) fresh beans, sting
removed, cut in half

2 cloves garlic, sliced

2 long red chilies, deseeded
and sliced

2–3 whole dried chilies

handful of curry leaves

juice of 1–2 lemons, to serve

Greek yogurt, to serve

Serves 4

Method

1. Add quinoa to a medium saucepan with the water. Bring to the boil, reduce heat and cover. Simmer for 10–15 minutes until all the water is absorbed. Remove from heat. Set aside for 10–15 minutes to cool.
2. Rub the tenderloins with a little oil, coat with the paprika and season with salt and pepper.
3. Heat oil in a large frying pan and cook the tenderloins on medium-high heat until golden on both sides and cooked. Remove from the pan and keep warm.
4. Toss the mustard and nigella seeds into the pan and cook on medium-high heat until they start to pop. Add a little more oil if needed.
5. Add the beans to the pan with garlic, sliced chilies, dried chilies and curry leaves and cook until fragrant about 1–2 minutes. Stir in the quinoa and season with salt to taste.
6. Arrange the tenderloins on top, cover, remove from the heat and leave to stand for about 5 minutes.
7. Serve with lemon juice and a side dish of yogurt.

Note: This is quite a spicy dish—add as much chili as you think you would prefer keeping in mind that the mustard seeds also have a little heat to them. "Nigella seeds" are used when pickling onions, can be tossed through steamed vegetables such as cabbage and add flavor to curries. They are also delicious when sprinkled on flat bread or Turkish bread. You can substitute with black sesame seeds, caraway seeds or cumin seeds.

Nasi Goreng

Ingredients

200 g (7 oz) quinoa, rinsed and drained

500 ml (16 fl oz) water

4 stalks Cavolo Nero kale

1–2 tablespoons extra virgin olive oil

300 g (10 oz) chicken breast fillets, trimmed and sliced into fine strips

1 onion, finely chopped

4 scallions (spring onions), sliced diagonally

1–2 long red chilies, deseeded and sliced

3 cloves garlic, finely chopped

8 large green prawns, peeled, deveined with tails intact

1–2 tablespoons sweet chili sauce

2 tablespoons kecap manis (sweet soy sauce)

2 tablespoons soy sauce

60 ml (2 fl oz) water

150 g (5 oz) bean sprouts

½ teaspoon extra virgin olive oil

4 free range eggs

1 lime, cut into wedges, to garnish

red chilies, sliced, to garnish

Serves 4

Method

1. Add quinoa to a medium saucepan with the water. Bring to the boil, reduce heat and cover. Simmer for 10–15 minutes until all the water is absorbed. Remove from heat. Allow to stand covered for 10–15 minutes. Set aside.

2. Thoroughly wash the kale, remove and discard most of the stalk and finely shred the leaves. Set aside.

3. Heat the oil in a large deep frying pan or a wok over medium to high heat. Add the chicken and cook until sealed. Remove from the pan and keep warm.

4. Add a little more oil to the pan if need be and sauté the onion, scallions and chilies until soft and golden. Stir in the garlic and cook for about another 30 seconds.

5. Add the prawns, chili sauce, kecap manis, soy sauce, kale and a little water to create some steam. Toss together and cook for about 3 minutes until the prawns start to turn pink and the kale has wilted. Stir in the quinoa, chicken and bean sprouts, remove from heat and set aside.

6. To cook eggs, heat oil to a frying pan. Crack eggs into the pan. If you are using a small pan, you may need to do a couple of eggs at a time.

7. Serve the quinoa with an egg on top and extra slices of chili, a sprinkling of soy sauce and wedges of lime.

Chicken and Spinach au Gratin

Ingredients

125 g (4 oz) quinoa, rinsed and drained

330 ml (11 fl oz) water

500 g (18 oz) chicken fillets, thigh or breasts

60 g (2 oz) butter

4 tablespoons quinoa flour

1–2 teaspoon English mustard

750 ml (24 fl oz) milk

90 g (3 oz) tasty cheese, grated

2 tablespoons Parmesan cheese, grated

150 g (5 oz) baby spinach leaves

salt and freshly ground black pepper

2 tablespoons tasty cheese, grated for topping

½–1 teaspoon ground paprika

Serves 4–6

Method

1. Preheat oven to 200°C (400°F) and line a baking tray with non-stick baking paper.
2. Place quinoa into a medium saucepan with the water. Bring to the boil, reduce the heat. Cover and simmer for 10–15 minutes or until all the water is absorbed. Leave to stand covered to cool completely while you prepare the rest of the dish.
3. Rub chicken fillets with a little olive oil and season with salt and pepper. Place on the baking tray and roast in the oven for 15–20 minutes until cooked.
4. Remove from oven, cover with foil and allow to rest for 5 minutes then chop into bite-sized pieces. Set aside.
5. Melt butter in a medium saucepan. Add the flour and stir to form a roux for about 1 minute to cook off the raw taste of the flour. Stir in the mustard and continue stirring.
6. Slowly pour in the milk and continue stirring until the mixture thickens and starts to bubble.
7. Stir in the cheeses and cook for another minute or so until cheese melts. Add the spinach and continue cooking until the spinach wilts.
8. Mix together the quinoa, chicken pieces and spinach sauce in a large bowl. Season with salt and pepper then transfer into a lightly-greased baking dish.
9. Sprinkle with the extra cheese and paprika and bake for about 20–30 minutes until golden before serving.

Shrimp and Chorizo Sausage
with Caramelized Lemons

Ingredients

250 g (9 oz) chorizo
  sausages, sliced
1 tablespoon extra virgin
  olive oil
3 cloves garlic, sliced
16 green shrimp (prawns),
  peeled, deveined, tail left
  intact
2 lemons, sliced and pips
  removed
1 large red onion, halved
  and finely sliced
300 g (10 oz) quinoa, rinsed
  and drained
pinch saffron
750 ml (24 fl oz) hot chicken
  stock
salt and pepper
6 scallions (spring onions),
  diagonally sliced into 5 cm
  (2 inch) pieces
3–4 tablespoons flat leaf
  parsley, chopped
juice of 1 lemon
extra flat leaf parsley,
  chopped, for garnish

Serves 4

Method

1. Heat a large non-stick deep frying pan over medium heat. Add the chorizo sausages and cook until golden— no need to add any oil as the chorizo will render its own fat. Remove sausage and set aside.
2. Pour oil into the same pan. Add the garlic and shrimp and cook until the shrimp turn red. Remove from the pan then add the lemon slices and cook until they become golden and caramelized. Remove and set aside.
3. Add the onion to the pan with a little more oil if necessary and sauté until soft.
4. Stir in the quinoa, saffron and stock. Bring to the boil, reduce heat, cover and simmer for about 12–14 minutes until all the liquid is absorbed.
5. When the quinoa is cooked, season with salt and pepper. Add scallions and parsley and cook for about 1 minute.
6. Toss the chorizo, shrimp and lemon juice through the quinoa until all ingredients are combined and the shrimp and chorizo are heated through.
7. Serve garnished with some extra chopped parsley.

Note: This is a very quick and easy dish to prepare especially for a light lunch with friends or family. You can always add more shrimp—this recipe has 4 per person.

Flakes

FLAKES

Spiced Almond and Chia Energy Bars

Raw Energy Bars

Quinoa, Chia and Coconut Porridge

Quinoa Breakfast Cereal Mix

Fruit and Nut Breakfast Porridge

Cherry, Orange and Chia Smoothie

Super Green Smoothie

Coconut Shrimp with Cilantro, Lime and Chili Mayonnaise

Flourless Pizza with Mozzarella, Tomatoes and Olives

Stuffed Mackerel with Sun-Dried Tomato, Basil and Olives

Lemon Garlic Crispy Fish Fillets

Parmesan and Herb Crumbed Chicken Tenderloins

Crumbed Chicken Tenderloins with Parmesan and Herbs

Chicken and Vegetable Loaf

Moroccan Stuffed Chicken

Baked Lamb Meatballs

Greek Lamb Cutlets with Minted Yogurt

Mustard Crusted Veal Schnitzel

Spiced Almond and Chia Energy Bars

Ingredients

60 g (2 oz) puffed quinoa
45 g (1½ oz) quinoa flakes
45 g (1½ oz) whole raw
   almonds with skin on
1 tablespoon sesame seeds
1 tablespoon chia seeds
3 tablespoons coconut sugar
2 tablespoons maple syrup
1 teaspoon cinnamon
¼ teaspoon nutmeg
pinch of ground cloves
1 egg white
1 teaspoon vanilla bean
   paste

Makes 12–15

Method

1. Preheat oven to 180°C (350°F) and line a 18 x 15 cm (7 x 6 inch) baking tray with non-stick baking paper and have paper come up the 2 longer sides of the tin for easy removal of the bars once cooked.
2. Mix together the puffed quinoa, quinoa flakes, almonds, sesame and chia seed, sugar, maple syrup and spices.
3. Stir in the egg white and vanilla paste and mix really well.
4. Place into prepared tin and bake for about 20 minutes until golden and set.
5. Cool in the tin for about 10 minutes then lift out and cut into bars and leave to cool completely.
6. Store in the refrigerator in an airtight container for about 3–4 days.

Raw Energy Bars

Ingredients

150 g (5 oz) Medjool dates,
    pitted
90 g (3 oz) unsalted cashews
60 ml (2 fl oz) maple syrup
1 teaspoon vanilla bean
    paste
90 g (3 oz) moist coconut
    flakes
45 g (1½ oz) quinoa flakes
60 g (2 oz) sultanas
60 g (2 oz) pepitas (pumpkin
    seeds)
45 g (1½ oz) sunflower seeds
60 ml (2 fl oz) coconut oil,
    melted

Makes 20–24

Method

1. Line the bottom of a 28 x 18 cm (11 x 7 inch) baking tin with non-stick paper. Make sure the paper comes up over the sides of the tin for easy removal of the bars.
2. Place the dates, cashews, maple syrup and vanilla into a food processor and process until you have a sticky paste with a little texture.
3. Transfer the date mixture to a bowl. Add all the other ingredients and mix well. You will need to use a wooden or metal spoon to mix this properly.
4. Spread the mixture into the prepared tin and use the back of a metal spoon to flatten and even out the mixture.
5. Cover with plastic wrap and refrigerate overnight.
6. Cut into small bars and keep in the refrigerator in a sealed container.

Note: You find this to be quite a sticky mixture when preparing it. Don't worry if it seems like it will never mix together properly—it will but you may need to use a little more elbow grease than usual.

These will keep stored in the refrigerator for up to 4 weeks or more.

Quinoa, Chia and Coconut Porridge

Ingredients

45 g (1½ oz) quinoa flakes
375 ml (12 fl oz) light
  coconut milk
125 ml (4 fl oz) water
2 tablespoons white chia
  seeds
2 tablespoons coconut or
  brown sugar
1 teaspoon vanilla bean
  paste
¼–½ teaspoon cinnamon
pinch of nutmeg
2 fresh bananas, sliced
  (optional)
extra coconut milk, to serve

Serves 2

Method

1. Place the quinoa flakes, milk, water, chia seeds, sugar, vanilla, cinnamon and nutmeg into a medium sized saucepan and stir well.
2. Bring to the boil on medium heat. Reduce the heat to low and simmer until thick and creamy, about 5 minutes.
3. Taste and adjust the level of sweetness to suit your taste. Place sliced bananas (if using) in serving bowls and spoon the porridge over.
4. Serve with extra coconut milk.

Note: You can substitute the coconut milk with any other milk that you prefer such as cow's milk, almond, soy or rice milk. Use other fruits if you wish.

Quinoa Breakfast Cereal Mix

Ingredients

150g (5 oz) red quinoa, rinsed and drained

375 ml (12 fl oz) water

125 g (4 oz) quinoa flakes

125 g (4 oz) whole blanched almonds

75 g (2½ oz) pepitas (pumpkin) seeds

75 g (2½ oz) sunflower seeds

60 g (2 oz) sesame seeds

2 teaspoons ground cinnamon

½ teaspoon ground nutmeg

1 tablespoon vanilla paste or extract

100 ml (2¾ fl oz) maple syrup

60 g (2 oz) light brown sugar, tightly packed

90 ml (3 fl oz) honey

2 tablespoons vegetable or extra light olive oil

150 g (5 oz) golden raisins

125 g (4 oz) dried cranberries

Makes about 1 kg (2 lbs)

Method

1. Place quinoa into a small saucepan with the water. Bring to the boil, reduce the heat and simmer for 10 minutes until all the water is absorbed. Remove from the heat, uncover and cool completely.
2. Preheat oven to 160°C (325°F) and line 2 large baking trays with non-stick baking paper.
3. In a large bowl mix together the quinoa flakes, cooled quinoa, almonds, pepitas, sunflower and sesame seeds, cinnamon and nutmeg.
4. Add the vanilla, maple syrup, brown sugar, honey and oil and mix really well as you want all the ingredients to be completely coated.
5. Spread the mixture out evenly over the 2 trays in a single layer and bake for about 30–40 minutes until crisp and crunchy and a rich golden color. Stir once or twice through the baking time making sure you keep the mix evenly distributed in the tray.
6. Remove from the oven and cool, then stir in the raisins and cranberries and when completely cold, store in an airtight container.
7. Serve with milk, or yogurt (or both) or sprinkle over porridge.

Note: This is one of those mixes that is good to have on hand. It is not only great for breakfast, you can grab a handful of this at anytime. Good in school or work lunches.

If you don't have maple syrup, golden syrup will work. Also, keep an eye on the mix while in the oven as it can burn easily. I have used the red quinoa in this recipe purely for the added crunch that you get from the darker seeds.

Fruit and Nut Breakfast Porridge

Ingredients

125 g (4 oz) quinoa grain, rinsed and drained

875 ml (28 fl oz) low fat milk

½–1 teaspoon ground cinnamon (optional)

45 g (1½ oz) quinoa flakes

60 g (2 oz) sultanas

45 g (1½ oz) apricots, chopped

2 tablespoons maple syrup or honey

45 g (1 ½ oz) almonds, skin on and roughly chopped

15 g (½ oz) sunflower seeds

30 g (1 oz) pepitas (pumpkin seeds)

2 teaspoons chia seeds

fresh raspberries, to serve

extra milk, to serve

unsweetened Greek yogurt, to serve

Serves 6

Method

1. Place quinoa into a medium to large sized saucepan with the milk and cinnamon if used. Bring to the boil reduce the heat, cover and simmer for 15 minutes with the lid slightly ajar as the milk can boil over during cooking.
2. Add the quinoa flakes, sultanas and apricots and simmer covered for another 5 minutes.
3. Remove from the heat and stir in the maple syrup or honey, almonds, sunflower seeds, pepitas and chia seeds.
4. Leave to stand for about 5 minutes then serve with extra milk and fresh raspberries or serve cold with yogurt stirred through and fresh raspberries.

Note: This is a thick and hearty porridge. You can serve it warm or cold. This is great as a breakfast on the go by mixing with unsweetened yogurt in small jars with a lid and taking to work or school. The porridge keeps well in the refrigerator for 4–5 days.

Cherry, Orange and Chia Smoothie

Ingredients

300 g (10 oz) frozen cherries
juice of 2 oranges
375 ml (12 fl oz) coconut
    water
2 tablespoons quinoa flakes
1 tablespoon maple syrup
1 tablespoon chia seeds
ice cubes (optional)
extra coconut water
    (optional)

Serves 4

Method

1. Place all ingredients into a blender and blend until thick, smooth and creamy.
2. Add some ice cubes or extra coconut water if you would like a thinner consistency.
3. Serve in individual glasses.

Note: This smoothie is gluten/wheat free. Vary the amount of sweetener to suit your taste and use berries or other fruit that are in season. If using fresh fruit, you may wish to add some ice cubes.

Super Green Smoothie

Ingredients

2 handfuls fresh kale

1 large green apple,
  unpeeled, core and seeds
  removed

30 g (1 oz) quinoa flakes

2 tablespoons honey or
  agave syrup

500 ml (16 fl oz) apple juice

2 celery stalks, roughly
  chopped

small handful fresh basil

juice of ½–1 lemon

2 tablespoons Greek yogurt
  (optional)

ice cubes

Serves 2

Method

1. Thoroughly wash the kale, remove and discard most of
    the stem and roughly chop the leaves.
2. Place kale and all other ingredients into a blender and
    blend until thick and smooth. If too thick, add a little
    water.

Note: You can vary the green leaves used according
to your taste. For example, you can use spinach and
cucumber instead of the kale. The yogurt tends to add a
little creamy richness to the drink however it tastes just as
good without yogurt if you would prefer to leave it out.

Coconut Shrimp with Cilantro, Lime and Chili Mayonnaise

Ingredients

60 g (2 oz) quinoa flour
salt and pepper
2 extra large eggs, lightly
    beaten
180 g (6 oz) moist coconut
    flakes
60 g (2 oz) quinoa flakes
24 large green shrimp
    (prawns), peeled,
    deveined, tails intact
2–3 tablespoons light olive
    oil, for frying
fresh cilantro (coriander), for
    garnish
lime wedges, to serve
extra cilantro (coriander)
    leaves, to serve

Mayonnaise

250 g (9 oz) whole egg
    mayonnaise
3–4 tablespoons fresh
    cilantro (coriander), finely
    chopped
1 long red chili, deseeded
    and finely chopped
juice of ½–1 lime

Serves 6

Method

1. Place the flour in a bowl and season with salt and pepper. Place the eggs in a separate bowl.
2. Mix together the coconut flakes and quinoa flakes and place in another bowl.
3. Rinse the shrimp under cold water then pat dry with paper towels to absorb moisture.
4. Coat the shrimp with seasoned flour then shake off any excess. Dip into the beaten eggs and then roll in the coconut mixture pressing quite firmly to coat well.
5. To make the mayonnaise, mix together the whole egg mayonnaise, cilantro, chilies and lime juice. Set aside in the refrigerator for at least an hour before using.
6. Add enough oil in a frying pan so that it will come half way up the thickness of each shrimp. Heat to medium-hot and cook the shrimp, a few at a time, until golden and crisp, about 2 minutes each side. Drain the shrimp on paper towels.
7. Serve with mayonnaise, lime wedges and a sprinkle of coriander leaves.

Note: This is a delicious dish and particularly impressive to prepare as a starter for a special occasion for friends or family—and it can be eaten by those who are gluten/wheat intolerant.

Flourless Pizza with Mozzarella, Tomatoes and Olives

Pizza Base

4 stalks kale

750 g (27 oz) cauliflower
   florets

2 tablespoons quinoa flakes

1 large clove garlic, finely
   grated

1 extra large egg

3 tablespoons Parmesan
   cheese, grated

Toppings

150 g (5 oz) tomato paste

1 clove garlic, finely grated

1 teaspoon dried oregano
   leaves

1 teaspoon extra virgin olive
   oil

4–6 mozzarella slices

10 grape tomatoes, halved

10–12 black olives

fresh rocket leaves, to
   garnish

Serves 2–4

Method

1. Thoroughly wash the kale, remove and discard the stem and roughly chop the leaves.
2. Place the cauliflower and kale into a food processor and process until very finely chopped.
3. Place on a large flat microwave safe dish. Cover with a silicon cover, plate or cling wrap and cook until the cauliflower and kale are very tender, about 8–10 minutes on high. Set aside to cool.
4. Place the kale and cauliflower mix into a fine sieve and squeeze out as much moisture as you can—your hands are best for this.
5. Preheat the oven to 200°C (400°F) fan forced. Line a 30 cm (12 inch) pizza tray with non-stick baking paper.
6. Combine the cauliflower and kale mix with the quinoa flakes, garlic, egg and Parmesan and mix well.
7. Spread the mixture onto the lined tray. Make the base a little thicker around the edge to form a crusty edge when cooked.
8. Bake for about 25–30 minutes until golden and crisp around the edges. Remove from the oven.
9. Mix together the tomato paste, garlic, oregano and oil and spread over the base of the pizza avoiding the edge.
10. Top with slices of mozzarella, tomatoes and olives.
11. Return to the oven and bake for a further 5–8 minutes until the mozzarella has melted.
12. Remove from the oven. Garnish with fresh rocket leaves and leave to rest and set for a few minutes before serving.

Note: This recipe is gluten/wheat free. It is not like your regular pizza base made with flour. This is very light, tasty and has a minimal amount of carbohydrates. Vary the toppings to suit your taste. If using a conventional oven, you may need to set the temperature a little higher and cook the base for a little longer.

Stuffed Mackerel with Sun-Dried Tomato, Basil and Olives

Ingredients

4 whole mackerel fish, scaled and gutted, about 350 g (12 oz) each
2 tablespoons fresh basil, finely chopped
60 g (2 oz) semi-dried tomatoes, chopped
60 g (2 oz) pitted Kalamata olives, chopped
2 large clove garlic, grated
1 lemon, zest and juice
1 teaspoon extra virgin olive oil
60 g (2 oz) quinoa flakes
salt and freshly cracked pepper
12 basil leaves
sliced garlic
extra basil leaves, for garnish
4 lemon wedges, to serve
rocket or baby spinach leaves, to serve

Serves 4

Method

1. Preheat the oven to 180°C (350°F). Line a baking tray or dish with non-stick baking paper.
2. Rinse the fish and pat dry with paper towels and remove as many of the bones from the fish as possible—mackerel have long thin bones that are very easy to pull out once the fish is gutted.
3. Make 3 small incisions across each fish diagonally.
4. Mix together the basil, sun-dried tomatoes, olives, garlic, lemon zest, juice and olive oil. Add the quinoa flakes and season with salt and pepper.
5. Divide mixture into 4 and fill each fish with this mixture.
6. Place the fish onto the prepared tray and place a basil leaf and slice of garlic in each incision. Drizzle with extra lemon juice and a little oil and bake for 15–20 minutes until the fish is cooked.
7. Remove from the oven and discard the basil leaves which would have by now almost disintegrated and replace with fresh leaves for garnish.
8. Serve with lemon wedges on a bed of rocket or fresh baby spinach.

Note: You can use this stuffing in any other fish of choice. Alternatively you can use the stuffing as a topping on fish fillets. Completely cover the fillets with the topping and bake as above.

Lemon Garlic Crispy Fish Fillets

Ingredients

150 g (5 oz) quinoa flakes
2–3 cloves garlic, finely
    grated
1 lemon, zest
2 tablespoons fresh chives,
    chopped
1–2 tablespoons flat leaf
    parsley, chopped
salt and freshly cracked
    black pepper
1 kg (2 lb 2 oz) fish fillets
60 g (2 oz) quinoa flour
2–3 eggs, lightly beaten
olive oil, for shallow frying
lemon wedges, to serve

Serves 4

Method

1. Combine the flakes with the garlic, lemon zest, chives and parsley. Season with salt and pepper and set aside.
2. Lightly dust each fillet with some quinoa flour, dip in a bowl of the beaten egg then press into the quinoa flake mixture to coat well.
3. Heat the oil in a large frying pan until hot and gently shallow fry the fish on a medium heat until golden, about 3–5 minutes each side depending on the thickness of the fish.
4. Remove from the pan and drain on paper towels.
5. Serve hot with lemon wedges and your salad of choice.

Note: This is a great way to get children to eat fish. My grandchildren and their friends love this recipe. To make it different for children, the fillets can be cut into thick strips to make fish fingers.

Crumbed Chicken Tenderloins with Parmesan and Herbs

Ingredients

1 kg (2 lb 2 oz) chicken
   breast tenderloins
150 g (5 oz) quinoa flakes
90 g (3 oz) Parmesan cheese,
   grated
1 tablespoon fresh thyme,
   chopped
1 tablespoon fresh chives,
   chopped
1 teaspoon flat leaf parsley,
   finely chopped
1 teaspoon sweet ground
   paprika
salt and freshly cracked
   black pepper
90 g (3 oz) quinoa flour
3 eggs, lightly beaten
olive oil, for shallow frying
lemon wedges, to serve
sweet Thai chili sauce
   (optional), to serve

Serves 6

Method

1. Trim any fat and small tendons from the tenderloins. Set aside.
2. Combine the quinoa flakes with the Parmesan, thyme, chives, parsley and paprika. Season with salt and pepper.
3. Lightly dust the tenderloins with a little flour. Dip into a bowl of the beaten egg to coat then press into the flake mixture to make sure the tenderloins are completely covered.
4. If possible refrigerate for half hour or longer before cooking to allow the crumbs to adhere to the tenderloins.
5. Heat the oil in a large frying pan on medium heat until hot. Gently shallow fry on each side until cooked and golden, about 3 minutes each side.
6. Test that they are cooked through by cutting one in the middle after cooking.
7. Serve with lemon wedges and a sweet Thai chili sauce if using.

Note: If you prefer you can leave out the herbs or substitute them with any other herbs of choice. I have found that kids love these—if you do have any leftovers, they make a great snack.

Chicken and Vegetable Loaf

Ingredients

500 g (1 lb) chicken breast
   mince
125 g (4 oz) corn kernels
1 medium courgette
   (zucchini), coarsely grated
60 g (2 oz), red peppers
   (capsicum), finely chopped
3 tablespoons quinoa flakes
2 cloves garlic, finely grated
4 scallions (spring onions),
   thinly sliced
1 tablespoon fresh parsley,
   finely chopped
1 teaspoon dried oregano
   leaves
1 teaspoon fresh thyme,
   finely chopped
2 eggs
salt and freshly ground
   pepper
quinoa flakes, to sprinkle

Serves 4–6

Method

1. Preheat oven to 180°C (350°F). Lightly oil a 31 x 11 x 7.5 cm (12 x 4½ x 3 inch) loaf tin and line the bottom with non-stick baking paper. Make sure the paper comes right up the longer sides of the tin for easy removal of the loaf once cooked.
2. Lightly oil the baking paper and sprinkle with the extra quinoa flakes.
3. Mix the chicken mince with the corn, courgette, peppers, quinoa flakes, garlic, scallions, parsley, thyme, oregano and eggs. Season with salt and pepper.
4. Make sure mixture is thoroughly combined. Place into the loaf tin, sprinkle with extra quinoa flakes and bake for about 40–45 minutes or until golden on top and the chicken is cooked.
5. Allow to cool in the tin for 5–10 minutes before lifting out and serving.

Note: This chicken loaf can be also eaten cold and makes a delicious sandwich filling. You can use chicken thigh or breast mince or even substitute with pork or turkey mince if you prefer.

Moroccan Stuffed Chicken

Ingredients

1 x 1.5 kg (3 lb) whole
   chicken
2 teaspoons ground cumin
1 teaspoon ground
   coriander
1 teaspoon ground turmeric
pinch cinnamon
3 tablespoons extra virgin
   olive oil
juice of 1 lemon
pinch of chili flakes
salt and pepper, to taste
60 g (2 oz) quinoa flakes
2 cloves garlic, grated
1 tablespoon grated fresh
   ginger
12 stuffed olives, thinly sliced
1½ tablespoons finely
   chopped preserved
   lemons
1 egg, lightly beaten
sweet paprika

Serves 4–6

Method

1. Preheat the oven to 200°C (400°F) and line a baking dish with non-stick baking paper.
2. Rinse chicken, remove any excess fat and pat dry with paper towels.
3. Mix together the cumin, coriander, turmeric, cinnamon, olive oil, lemon juice and chili flakes. Season with salt and pepper, set aside.
4. In another bowl, combine quinoa flakes with garlic, ginger, olives, preserved lemons and salt and pepper.
5. Rub some of the spice mix over the chicken including inside the cavity.
6. Pour remaining spice mix into the flake mixture with the egg and mix well to make the stuffing.
7. Stuff the chicken with the mixture and secure the opening with a small metal skewer.
8. Place into the prepared dish. Drizzle a little extra oil and lemon juice, sprinkle with sweet paprika and season with more salt and pepper.
9. Pour some water in the bottom of the dish and bake for about 1 –1¼ hours until the chicken is golden and cooked through.
10. Remove from oven, cover with foil and leave to rest for about 15 minutes.
11. Slice and serve with your favorite salad.

Baked Lamb Meatballs

Ingredients

Minted Yogurt
250 g (9 oz) low fat yogurt
2 tablespoons mint, finely
  chopped
salt and pepper
1 small clove garlic, finely
  grated (optional)

Meatballs
500 g (1 lb 1 oz) lamb mince
2 cloves garlic, grated
1 onion, grated
4 scallions (spring onions),
  finely sliced
½ teaspoon smoked paprika
1 teaspoon dried oregano
rind of 1 lemon
1 tablespoon lemon juice
2 tablespoons flat leaf
  parsley, finely chopped
1 extra large egg
salt and freshly cracked
  black pepper
60 g (2 oz) quinoa flakes

Makes about 20

Method

1. Preheat the oven to 200°C (400°F) and line a baking tray with non-stick baking paper.
2. To make the yogurt, mix all the ingredients together and refrigerate for half an hour before serving.
3. Place the lamb mince in a bowl with the garlic, onion, scallions, paprika, oregano, lemon rind and juice, parsley and egg. Season with salt and pepper to taste. Add the quinoa flakes and mix well.
4. Shape mixture into balls the size of a large walnut and place onto the prepared tray. Bake for 12–15 minutes until cooked and browned.
5. Serve with the minted yogurt.

Note: These are also delicious eaten cold—great for picnics and sandwich fillings.

Greek Lamb Cutlets with Minted Yogurt

—+····❃····+—

Ingredients

12 lamb cutlets
1 lemon, juice and zest
2 teaspoons extra virgin
   olive oil
125 g (4 oz) quinoa flakes
2–3 cloves garlic, finely
   grated
1 tablespoon dried oregano
   leaves
salt and pepper
lemon wedges, to serve

Minted Yogurt

250 ml (9 fl oz) unsweetened
   Greek yogurt
1 tablespoon mint, finely
   chopped
1 small clove garlic, finely
   grated
salt and pepper

Serves 4–6

Method

1. Lightly coat the cutlets with a little of the lemon juice and olive oil, rubbing well into the meat.
2. Mix the quinoa flakes with the garlic, oregano, lemon zest and juice and olive oil. Season with salt and pepper.
3. Rub the flakes really well with the other ingredients so that they are all evenly combined and you have a moist mixture.
4. Press the cutlets firmly into the quinoa mixture to cover completely,
5. To make the minted yogurt, mix together the yogurt, mint and garlic. Season with salt and pepper. For a deep colored, velvety smooth sauce, mix in a food processor or blender.
6. Heat enough olive oil in a large frying pan on medium-high heat until hot but not burning. Shallow fry the cutlets, cooking on each side until golden, about 2–3 minutes. Drain on paper towels.
7. Serve with wedges of lemon and the minted yogurt.

Note: These lamb chops are always a huge hit—there are rarely any leftovers.

Mustard Crusted Veal Schnitzel

Ingredients

4 veal steaks, about 500 g
  (1 lb 1 oz) in total
125 g (4 oz) quinoa flakes
1–2 tablespoons whole grain
  mustard
1 lemon, zest
2 tablespoons flat leaf
  parsley, finely chopped
salt and freshly cracked
  black pepper
3 tablespoon quinoa flour
2 extra large eggs, lightly
  beaten
extra virgin olive oil, for
  shallow frying
lemon wedges, to serve

Serves 4

Method

1. Lightly pound the steaks with a mallet or rolling pin and set aside.
2. Add quinoa flakes, mustard, lemon zest and parsley to a bowl. Season with salt and pepper. Rub the mustard and lemon rind into the flakes so that they are evenly distributed.
3. Dust each veal steak with quinoa flour then dip into the beaten egg until well coated. Press firmly into the flake mixture making sure that all the steaks are evenly and well coated. If the steaks are too big, cut them in half before you start this crumbing process.
4. Heat some olive oil in a large frying pan until hot but not burning hot over medium heat and shallow fry the steaks, without crowding the pan, until golden, about 2–3 minutes on each side. Drain on kitchen paper.
5. Serve with lemon wedges.

Note: Thin slices of pork or chicken can be used instead of the veal.

Flour

FLOUR

Fresh Quinoa Pasta Dough

Ginger Bread

Spinach and Feta Cheese Pots

Quinoa Crackes with Red Kidney Bean Dip

Savory Herb and Pamesan Cheese Crackers

Pea and Asparagus Quiche

Shrimp and Watercress Bake

Chocolate Orange Cake

Banana and Maple Syrup Hotcakes

Chocolate and Cranberry Slice

Orange and Cranberry Mini Bundt Cakes

Chocolate Chip Muffins

Fresh Quinoa Pasta Dough

Ingredients
500 g (1 lb 1 oz) quinoa flour
½ teaspoon salt
5 extra large eggs
1 tablespoon extra virgin
   olive oil

Serves 4

Method
1. Place all of the ingredients into a food process and process until all the ingredients come together into a ball.
2. It may seem that the processor is going forever and nothing is happening but the mix will eventually come together and you won't have to wait all that long. Form into a ball.
3. Knead for a few minutes then using a pasta maker, roll out and shape into your favorite pasta. Set aside.
4. Bring a pot of salted water to the boil. Cook the pasta for 3–5 minutes.
5. Drain the pasta and toss with your favorite sauce.
6. Serve immediately.

Note: There is no need to rest pasta in the refrigerator before shaping although you can if you are preparing the pasta dough in advance. This goes well with any pasta sauce and lots of grated Parmesan or Romano cheese.

Ginger Bread

Ingredients

150 g (4 oz) quinoa flour
1 tablespoon ground ginger
1 teaspoon cinnamon
1 teaspoon baking powder
1 teaspoon baking soda (bicarbonate of soda)
½ teaspoon salt
125 g (4 oz) unsalted butter, melted
125 ml (4 fl oz) maple syrup
90 g (3 oz) coconut sugar
90 g (3 oz) stem ginger in syrup, chopped into small pieces
2 eggs
1 teaspoon vanilla bean paste
1 cup sour cream
1–2 tablespoons syrup (from stem ginger
sprinkle confectioners' (icing) sugar (optional), for dusting

Serves 8–10

Method

1. Preheat oven to 180°C (350 °F). Lightly grease a 26 x 15 cm (10 x 6 inch) loaf tin and line with non-stick baking paper making sure it is long enough to come overhang two ends of the tin so it is easy to lift out when cooked.
2. Sift together the quinoa flour, ground ginger, cinnamon, baking powder, baking soda and salt into a large bowl.
3. Add the butter, maple syrup and coconut sugar to a small saucepan and stir over low heat until the butter and sugar have melted and the mixture is smooth. Keep an eye on it as the coconut sugar can burn easily.
4. Allow to slightly cool then pour into the flour mixture. Add the stem ginger to the mixture with the eggs, vanilla and sour cream. Stir well with a spatula to combine the ingredients together.
5. Pour the mixture into the prepared tin and bake for about 45–50 minutes or until a skewer comes out clean when tested.
6. Brush the top with some of the ginger syrup as soon as it comes out of the oven then allow to cool in tin for about 10 minutes before lifting out onto a wire rack to cool completely. Dust with confectioners' sugar if desired.

Note: This ginger bread is delicious served warm with a cup of tea or as a dessert with a dollop of vanilla ice-cream. It is just as delicious served cold.

Spinach and Feta Cheese Pots

Ingredients

2½ tablespoons extra virgin
olive oil
1 onion, finely chopped
2 cloves garlic, finely
chopped
60 gm (2 oz) sun-dried
tomatoes, finely chopped
250 g (9 oz) fresh baby
spinach leaves
150 g (4 oz) feta cheese
2 tablespoons Parmesan
cheese, grated
2 extra large eggs, lightly
beaten
60 ml (2 fl oz) milk
2½ tablespoons extra virgin
olive oil
125 g (4 oz) quinoa flour
1 teaspoon baking powder
freshly cracked black pepper

Serves 8

Method

1. Preheat the oven to 200°C (400°F), fan forced. Line 8
   stainless steel baking pots (or 8-cup muffin tray) with
   baking paper.
2. Heat 2 tablespoons of oil in a large frying pan and sauté
   the onion until soft and golden. Stir in the garlic and cook
   for another 30 seconds or so.
3. Add the sun-dried tomatoes and cook for 1 minute. Add
   spinach and keep turning it over in the pan until it wilts.
   Don't be alarmed as you start off with what looks like a
   mountain of spinach—once it wilts, it will be reduce to a
   small amount.
4. Once wilted, cook the spinach for about 1 minute.
   Transfer into a bowl.
5. Crumble the feta cheese into the same bowl, add the
   Parmesan and eggs and mix well then mix in the milk and
   ½ tablespoon of oil.
6. Stir in the flour and baking powder, season with black
   pepper and lightly mix to combine.
7. Divide mixture into 8 and fill baking pots. Place on
   a baking tray and place in the oven for about 15–20
   minutes, or until set and golden on top.
8. Serve with a salad or seasonal vegetables of choice.

Note: For something a little different, terracotta flower
pots look terrific when you serve this in the pots on plates
surrounded by a big garden salad or vegetables. Each pot
holds about 125 ml (4 fl oz).

   If you prefer, you can substitute the feta with a soft
goat's cheese.

Quinoa Crackers
with Red Kidney Bean Dip

Red Kidney Bean Dip

1 x 400g (14 oz) tin red kidney
  beans, drained
2 cloves of garlic, chopped
4 scallions (spring onions),
  chopped
1 green chili, deseeded and
  roughly chopped
1–2 tablespoons extra virgin
  olive oil
1 teaspoon ground cumin
½ teaspoon ground coriander
½ teaspoon ground paprika
3–4 tablespoons fresh cilantro
  (coriander), chopped
juice of ½ –1 lime
salt and freshly ground black
  pepper
extra virgin olive oil, to serve

Quinoa Crackers

250 g (4 oz) quinoa flour
1 teaspoon gluten-free baking
  powder
250 g (4 oz) quinoa flakes
1 teaspoon sea salt
1 teaspoon ground cumin
1 teaspoon sweet paprika
3 teaspoons coconut oil or
  extra virgin olive oil
125 ml (4 fl oz) warm water

Makes 30

Method

1. To make the red kidney dip, place all ingredients
    except the cilantro into a food processor or blender
    and pulse until you have a soft puréed mixture with a
    little texture.
2. Stir in the cilantro and lime juice to suit your taste.
    Season with salt and pepper. Refrigerate for at least 2–3
    hours before serving.
3. Preheat oven to 180°C (350°F) and line 2 baking trays
    with non-stick baking paper.
4. To make the crackers, sift quinoa flour and baking
    powder into a bowl. Stir in the quinoa flakes, salt, cumin
    and paprika.
5. Mix in the coconut oil and enough warm water to bind
    the dough together.
6. Form the dough into a ball and then using a floured
    rolling pin, roll out thinly onto a sheet of baking paper.
    Cut into cracker-sized, desired shapes.
7. Place the shapes onto the prepared baking trays and
    bake for about 10–12 minutes until golden. Keep an
    eye on them as they can burn fairly quickly—ideally
    they should not be too soft when they come out of the
    oven. Cool completely on the tray.
8. Serve the dip with a drizzle of extra virgin olive oil and
    the crackers on the side.

Savory Herb
and Parmesan Cheese Crackers

Ingredients

125 g (4 oz) butter, room
  temperature
90 g (3 oz) Parmesan cheese,
  grated
1 tablespoon fresh thyme
  leaves, chopped
1 tablespoon fresh chives,
  chopped
1 clove garlic, finely grated
½ teaspoon ground paprika
freshly cracked black pepper
125 g (4 oz) quinoa flour
½ teaspoon baking powder
½ teaspoon baking soda
  (bicarbonate of soda)

Makes about 16

Method

1. Using an electric mixer, cream the butter until light and fluffy. Add the Parmesan cheese, thyme, chives, garlic paprika and a good grind of pepper. Mix well to combine.
2. Sift together the flour, baking powder and baking soda.
3. Slowly add the flour to the butter mixture and mix until you have a dough that holds together.
4. Shape the dough into a log about 20 cm (8 inch) long. Wrap in plastic and freeze for about 1 hour or until required. If the dough is rock hard, let it thaw until you can easily cut with a serrated knife but don't allow to come to room temperature completely.
5. Preheat oven to 180°C (350°F) and line a baking tray with non-stick baking paper.
6. Cut the log of dough into rounds and place on the prepared baking tray. Bake in the oven for 10–15 minutes until golden.
7. Cool on the baking tray and then a wire rack. Store in an airtight container for up to 4 days.

Note: These savory crackers (biscuits) are great to serve to guests with a cold drink. They are gluten/wheat free.

Pea and Asparagus Quiche

Ingredients

2 tablespoons extra virgin
   olive oil
1 onion, finely chopped
2 cloves garlic, finely
   chopped
500 g (18 oz) fresh asparagus
250 g (9 oz) frozen baby peas
6 extra large eggs
300 ml (10 fl oz) milk
200 ml (7 fl oz) cream
75 g (2½ oz) quinoa flour
60 g (2 oz) mature cheese,
   grated
2 tablespoons Parmesan
   cheese, grated
salt and freshly cracked
   black pepper

Serves 6

Method

1. Preheat oven to 180°C (350°F) and lightly grease a 30 x 5 cm (12 x 2 inch) round quiche dish.
2. Heat the oil in a large frying pan and sauté the onion until golden and soft.
3. Trim the asparagus and discard tough bottom part then chop into pieces, reserve the tips to use as garnish.
4. Add the garlic and asparagus (not the tips) to the pan and cook for about 4–5 minutes, stirring regularly until the asparagus is tender. Stir in the peas and cook for 3–4 minutes until they defrost. Set aside to cool.
5. Whisk together the eggs, milk and cream. Slowly incorporate the flour into the egg mixture then stir in the cheeses. Season with salt and pepper to taste keeping in mind the saltiness of the cheese.
6. Line the bottom of the quiche dish with the asparagus and peas then pour over the egg mixture. Stir lightly to incorporate.
7. Arrange the reserved asparagus tips on the top and bake for about 30–40 minutes until the pie has set and the top is golden.
8. Serve with a salad of choice.

Shrimp and Watercress Bake

Ingredients

150 g (5 oz) quinoa, rinsed and drained
375 ml (12 fl oz) water
2 tablespoons butter or ghee
1 small onion, finely chopped
2 cloves garlic, finely chopped
1 teaspoon curry powder
½ teaspoon garam masala
3 tablespoons quinoa flour
575 ml (18 fl oz) milk, room temperature
1 lemon or lime, rind
salt and pepper
500 g (1 lb 1 oz) small shrimp (prawns), cooked, shelled and deveined
2 handfuls fresh watercress, roughly chopped
2–3 tablespoons fresh chives, chopped
extra chives, for garnish
lemon or lime juice, to serve

Serves 4

Method

1. Place quinoa in a small saucepan with the water. Bring to the boil, reduce the heat and cover. Simmer for 10–15 minutes until all the water is absorbed. Remove from the heat and leave to rest covered for 10–15 minutes while you prepare the rest of the recipe.
2. Preheat oven to 200°C (400°F) and lightly grease a 22 x 28 cm (8½ x 11 inch) baking dish.
3. Melt butter or ghee in a saucepan. Add the onion and garlic and cook until soft and golden. Add the curry powder and garam masala and cook for a few seconds. Stir in the flour to form a roux and cook for about 1 minute. Slowly add the milk, stirring constantly until the sauce starts to thicken and bubble.
4. Season with salt and a good grind of pepper then stir in most of the shrimp (leave some for garnish). Cook over gentle heat for about 1 minute. Mix in the cooked quinoa and watercress and pour into greased dish. Arrange the remaining shrimp on top and garnish with the chives. Bake for about 25–30 minutes until golden.
5. Remove from oven and set aside to cool for about 10–15 minutes before serving with a squeeze of lemon or lime, seasonal vegetables or a salad.

Note: You can substitute the watercress with rocket or peas.

Chocolate Orange Cake

Ingredients

45 g (1½ oz) raw cacao powder, sifted

1 teaspoon instant coffee powder

6 tablespoons hot water

125 g (4 oz) butter at room temp

125 g (4 oz) superfine (caster) sugar

2 large eggs

1 teaspoon vanilla bean paste

1 orange, juice and rind

125 g (4 oz) quinoa flour

1½ teaspoons baking powder

½ teaspoon baking soda (bicarbonate of soda)

Orange Icing

90 g (3 oz) pure confectioners' (icing sugar), sifted

1 tablespoon orange juice

1 teaspoon orange rind, very finely grated

Serves 6–8

Method

1. Preheat oven to 180°C (350 °F) and grease a 20 cm (8 in) bundt cake tin.
2. Mix together the raw cacao, coffee and enough hot water to make a thick paste. Set aside.
3. Beat butter and sugar with electric beaters until light and fluffy then beat in the eggs, cacao mixture, vanilla paste, orange juice and rind.
4. Sift together the flour, baking powder and baking soda then, using a rubber spatula, fold into the cacao mixture. Combine thoroughly. The mixture should feel very light and have the texture of mousse.
5. Pour into the prepared tin and bake for about 30 minutes until a skewer comes out clean when tested.
6. Cool in the tin for about 10 minutes before turning out on to a wire rack to cool completely.
7. To prepare the icing, whisk all the ingredients together until you have a thick, smooth consistency. Drizzle the cake with icing.

Note: This is quite a moist cake. It keeps well in the refrigerator. If you would prefer not to use the icing, just dust the cake with sifted cacao powder or plain icing sugar.

Banana and Maple Syrup Hotcakes

Ingredients

2 ripe bananas, mashed
1 teaspoon lemon juice
125 g (4 oz) quinoa flour
1 teaspoon baking powder
1 teaspoon baking soda
   (bicarbonate of soda)
2 tablespoons maple syrup
2 extra large eggs
1½ teaspoons vanilla extract
300 ml (10¼ fl oz) buttermilk
butter, for cooking
maple syrup, to serve

Makes about 12

Method

1. Combine the bananas with the lemon juice and set aside.
2. Sift together the quinoa flour, baking powder and baking soda.
3. Whisk together the maple syrup, eggs and vanilla, and then mix in the buttermilk.
4. Gently fold together the dry ingredients with the wet ingredients until you have a lump-free smooth batter. Stir in the bananas.
5. Heat a little butter in a non-stick pan on low heat until it bubbles. Pour about 60 g (2 oz) of the hotcake (pancake) mixture into the pan and form a round shape.
6. Cook until bubbles form on top, gently flip and cook on the other side for about 30 seconds.
7. Remove from pan and repeat with the remaining batter.
8. Serve hotcakes stacked on top of one another with a drizzle of maple syrup.

Note: These hotcakes are light and delicate. They need a some gentle care when flipping over. Keep an eye on the heat so that they don't burn.

Chocolate and Cranberry Slice

Ingredients

125 g (4 oz) quinoa flour
1 teaspoon baking powder
¼ teaspoon salt
60 g (2 oz) dried cranberries
60 g (2 oz) dark chocolate
  chips
60 g (2 oz) white chocolate
  chips
125 g (4 oz) butter, melted
75 g (2½ oz) caster sugar
1 extra large egg
2 teaspoons vanilla bean
  paste
80 ml (2½ fl oz) milk

White Chocolate Icing

60 g (3 oz) white chocolate

Makes 12

Method

1. Preheat the oven to 160°C (325°F) and line the bottom of a 20 cm (8 inch) square slice tin with non-stick baking paper.
2. Sift flour, baking powder and salt together into a bowl. Add cranberries and chocolate chips. Set aside.
3. Mix together the melted butter and sugar in a separate bowl until light and fluffy. Mix in the egg and vanilla then stir in the milk. Gently fold through the flour mixture with a rubber spatula.
4. Pour the mixture into the prepared tin and bake for 20–25 minutes until golden and a metal skewer comes out clean when tested. Cool completely. before drizzling with the melted chocolate.
5. To make the icing, put chopped chocolate in a heatproof bowl that fits over a pot of barely simmering water (water bath method). Stir occasionally until the chocolate has melted. Remove from heat. Make sure not to let the water come in contact with the chocolate. Also, be sure the bowl and spoon or spatula are perfectly dry.
6. Drizzle the melted chocolate over the slice with a teaspoon. Allow to set and cut into slices.

Note: You can choose to omit the chocolate icing as these chocolate cranberry slices are just as delicious without it.

Orange and Cranberry Mini Bundt Cakes

Ingredients

60 g (2 oz) quinoa flour
90 g (3 oz) coconut sugar
1 teaspoon baking powder
150 g (5 oz) almond meal
125 g (4 oz) dried cranberries
1 orange, zest and juice
125 g (4 oz) unsalted butter,
  melted and cooled
1 teaspoon vanilla extract
4 large egg whites

Orange Icing

1 tablespoon confectioner's
  (icing) sugar, sifted
1 tablespoon orange juice

Makes 12 cakes

Method

1. Preheat oven to 180°C (350°F). Grease a 12-cup mini bundt cake tin with butter.
2. Sift the quinoa flour, sugar and baking powder into a bowl then mix in the almond meal breaking up any lumps in the mixture with a fork.
3. Add the cranberries and orange zest to the mixture then lightly stir in the orange juice, butter and vanilla.
4. Beat the egg whites to form foamy and soft peaks then gently fold into the mixture. Spoon the mixture evenly into the prepared cake tins.
5. Bake for until golden brown and cooked when tested with a metal skewer, about 15 minutes.
6. Remove from the oven and leave for 10 minutes before removing from the cake tins and cooling completely on a wire rack.
7. To make the icing, mix the icing sugar with enough orange juice to make the icing a slightly thick but still runny consistency.
8. When the cakes have cooled, drizzle the top of each one with a little of the orange icing.

Note: A bundt cake tin has rings embedded to create a pattern on the cake when it is turned out. A 12-cup muffin tin works just as well.

Chocolate Chip Muffins

Ingredients

150 g (5 oz) quinoa flour
125 g (4 oz) coconut sugar
45 g (1½ oz) raw cacao
  powder
1 level teaspoon baking
  soda (bicarbonate of soda)
1½ level teaspoon gluten-
  free baking powder
⅛ teaspoon salt
125g (4ozs) chocolate chips,
180 ml (6 fl oz) milk
2 extra large eggs
2 teaspoons vanilla paste or
  extract
60 ml (2 fl oz) vegetable or
  grapeseed oil

Makes 12

Method

1. Preheat oven to 180°C (350°F) and line a 12-cup muffin tin with paper cases.
2. Sift together flour, sugar, cacao, baking soda, baking powder and salt into a large bowl then stir through the chocolate chips.
3. Pour milk into a jug then lightly beat in the eggs, vanilla and oil.
4. Make a well in the middle of the dry ingredients and slowly pour in the liquid ingredients mixing as you go until all the ingredients are combined.
5. Spoon the mixture evenly into the prepared muffin tins and bake for about 15 minutes until the muffins are firm to the touch and skewer comes out clean when tested.

Note: These muffins are great for school lunches. Keep in mind that raw cacao can be quite bitter. You can substitute the coconut sugar with soft brown sugar.

Puffed

PUFFED

Salmon and Potato Cakes

Fruit and Almond Bars

Chocolate, Chia and Coconut Power Balls

Banana, Chia and Dried Fruit Slice

Cranberry and Orange Snack Balls

Ginger and Raisin Bites

Date and Ginger Cookies

Carob Squares

Quinoa and Dried Fruit Yogurt Topping

Maple Syrup, Coconut and Quinoa Cookies

Raw Cacao and Coconut Crackles

Ice-Cream Balls

Rocky Road

Salmon and Potato Cakes

Ingredients

750 g (27 oz) desiree
   potatoes, peeled
4 x 500 g (18 oz) salmon
   fillets
salt and freshly cracked
   black pepper
1–2 tablespoons extra virgin
   olive oil
4 scallions (spring onions),
   finely sliced
2 cloves garlic, finely chop
zest of 1 lemon
2 tablespoons dill, finely
   chopped
30 g (1 oz) puffed quinoa
2 tablespoons popped
   quinoa
olive oil cooking spray
baby rocket, to serve
grape tomatoes, to serve
lemon juice, to serve

Serves 4

Method

1. Cook the potatoes in salted boiling water until tender. As soon as they are cooked, mash finely and keep warm.
2. Preheat the oven to 200°C (400°F) fan forced and line a large baking tray with non-stick baking paper.
3. Place salmon on the prepared tray, skin side down, season with salt and pepper and drizzle with a little olive oil.
4. Bake for about 12–15 minutes until cooked. Remove from oven and set aside. Leave oven on and line another tray with non-stick baking paper.
5. Heat the remaining oil in a large frying pan and sauté the scallions until soft and golden. Add the garlic and cook for about 30 seconds, remove from the heat and stir in the lemon zest and dill.
6. Add the puffed quinoa to a dry frying pan over medium heat until golden and aromatic. Set aside.
7. Remove skin from the salmon and discard. Flake the salmon into small pieces. Add to the potatoes with the toasted puffed quinoa and scallions. Season with salt and pepper to taste and mix well.
8. Divide mixture into 8 portions and shape into round cakes then roll in the popped quinoa to cover completely.
9. Place onto the second prepared baking tray. Spray liberally with the cooking oil spray and bake for 20–25 minutes or until golden.
10. Serve on a bed of fresh baby rocket and tiny tomatoes and lots of lemon juice.

Fruit and Almond Bars

Ingredients

60 g (2 oz) quinoa flakes

40 g (1½ oz) red quinoa grain, rinsed and drained

90 g (3 oz) natural whole almonds with skin on, cut into pieces

1 teaspoon coconut oil

30 g (1 oz) shredded coconut

40 g (1½ oz) puffed quinoa

40 g (1½ oz) pepitas (pumpkin seeds)

40 g (1½ oz) dried apricots, chopped

40 g (1½ oz) cranberries

60 g (2 oz) golden raisins (sultanas)

3 tablespoons honey or maple syrup

½ orange, juice and zest

3 tablespoons organic coconut oil, melted

3 extra large egg whites, lightly whisked

Makes about 16

Method

1. Preheat oven to 180°C (350°F) and line a baking tray with non-stick baking paper.
2. Place flakes, grain and almonds onto the baking tray and coat with the 1 teaspoon of coconut oil then toast in the oven stirring once or twice. Cook for about 7–10 minutes until golden.
3. Remove from the oven and place into a large mixing bowl then add the coconut, puffed quinoa, pepitas, apricots, cranberries and raisins and give them a good mix.
4. Stir in some of the honey or maple syrup and taste the mixture at this stage to check the level of sweetness. Adjust accordingly.
5. Reduce the oven temperature to 160°C (325°F) and line a 29 x 19 x 4 cm (11½ x 7½ x 1½ inch) baking tin with non-stick baking paper leaving a good over-hang of paper on the sides so that the fruity bars can lifted out easily.
6. Stir in the egg whites and coconut oil and mix well so that all the ingredients are thoroughly coated in the oil and egg whites.
7. Press mixture into the second prepared baking tin and bake for about 20 minutes until firm to the touch and lightly golden.
8. Allow to cool in the tray for 10 minutes before cutting into desired bar sizes then cool completely in the tin. Remove and wrap each bar individually with greaseproof paper and store in an airtight container.

Chocolate, Chia and Coconut Power Balls

Ingredients

60 g (2 oz) almonds, with skin on

125 g (4 oz) Medjool dates, pitted

3 tablespoons organic raw cacao powder

2 tablespoons organic raw coconut oil, melted

2 tablespoons maple syrup

1 large orange, zest and juice

3 tablespoons orange juice

2 tablespoons chia seeds

30 g (1 oz) puffed quinoa

60 g (2 oz) moist coconut flakes or shredded coconut

Makes 12

Method

1. Place the almonds in a food processor and process until finely chopped.
2. Add the dates, cacao powder, coconut oil, maple syrup, zest and orange juice. Process until the mixture comes together and you have a paste-like mixture. If the mixture is too thick and not processing smoothly, add a little more orange juice to loosen.
3. Transfer mixture into a bowl. Stir in the chia seeds and puffed quinoa.
4. Mix all the ingredients together until well combined, pressing as you mix so that the mixture holds together. Taste for sweetness and add a little more maple syrup if desired.
5. Wet the palms of your hands with a little cold water and roll the mixture into walnut-sized balls or whatever size you prefer.
6. Refrigerate for at least 3–4 hours before serving.

Note: Store these in the refrigerator in an airtight container for 3–4 weeks. I like to wrap these individually in cellophane paper and keep them in the refrigerator ready to go.

Banana, Chia and Dried Fruit Slice

Ingredients

2 bananas, mashed
1 orange, zest and juice
½ teaspoon baking soda
   (bicarbonate of soda)
125 g (4 oz) butter, melted
150 g (5 oz) coconut sugar
60 ml (2 fl oz) maple syrup or
   honey
1 teaspoon vanilla bean
   paste
1 teaspoon baking powder
60 g (2 oz) puffed quinoa
45 g (1½ oz) quinoa flakes
180 g (6 oz) mixed dried fruit
60 g (2 oz) dried cranberries
60 g (2 oz) pepitas (pumpkin
   seeds)
2 tablespoons sesame seeds
2 tablespoons chia seeds

Makes 16

Method

1. Preheat the oven to 160°C (325°F) and line a 20 cm
    (8 inch) square baking tin with baking paper. Leave an
    overhang of paper on 2 sides of the tin for easy lifting the
    bars out of the tin.
2. Finely mash the banana and stir in the zest, juice and
    baking soda. Mix well and set aside.
3. Mix together the butter, coconut sugar, maple syrup and
    vanilla. Set aside.
4. Place all other ingredients into a large bowl and mix well.
    Fold in the banana and butter mixture and mix well to
    combine.
5. Spread the fruit mixture into the prepared tin. Flatten and
    smooth with the back of a spoon and bake until golden
    and set, about 40 minutes.
6. Cool completely in the tin before cutting into squares or
    bars. Store in the refrigerator in a sealed container.

Note: These fruit bars are soft and chewy and are best
kept in the refrigerator. They will keep for about 4–5 days.

Cranberry and Orange Snack Balls

Ingredients

125 g (4 oz) raw almonds
125 g (4 oz) dried cranberries
90 g (3 oz) crimson or golden
  raisins (sultanas)
1 teaspoon fresh orange zest
1 teaspoon vanilla bean
  paste
2–3 tablespoons organic raw
  coconut oil, melted
1 tablespoon puffed quinoa

Makes 12

Method

1. Place almonds into a food processor and process until very finely chopped.
2. Add the cranberries, raisins, orange zest, vanilla and coconut oil and continue processing until the nuts and fruit are all finely chopped and you have a slightly sticky mixture with a little texture to it.
3. Transfer this mixture into a bowl and mix in the puffed quinoa. Mix well pressing the mixture so that it holds firmly together—your hands are probably best for this.
4. Roll the mixture into balls the size of a walnut or a size that best suits you and refrigerate until set.
5. Store the snack balls in an airtight container in the refrigerator for up 1–2 weeks.

Ginger and Raisin Bites

Ingredients

100 g (3½ oz) unsalted
  cashews
100 g (3½ oz) glace ginger
125 g (4 oz) crimson or
  golden raisins (or sultanas)
2 teaspoons raw cacao
  powder
2 tablespoons organic raw
  coconut oil, melted
30 g (1 oz) puffed quinoa

Makes 18

Method

1. Place cashews into a food processor and process until finely chopped. Add the ginger, raisins, cacao and coconut oil and continue processing until the nuts and fruit are all finely chopped and you have a slightly sticky mixture with a little texture to it.
2. Transfer this mixture into a bowl and mix in the quinoa puffs. Mix all the ingredients together really well. Your hands are probably best for this.
3. Press the mixture as you mix so that it holds together firmly.
4. With slightly wet hands, roll the mixture into bite sized rounds or a size that best suits you and refrigerate until set.

Note: These bites will keep in the refrigerator in an airtight container for at least 3–4 weeks.

Date and Ginger Cookies

Ingredients

150 g (5 oz) unsalted butter

4 tablespoons coconut sugar

2 extra large eggs

2 teaspoons vanilla extract

90 g (3 oz) quinoa flour

2 teaspoons ground ginger

1 teaspoon gluten-free
baking powder

½ teaspoon baking soda
(bicarbonate of soda)

30 g (1 oz) quinoa flakes

90 g (3 oz) dried dates,
chopped

4 tablespoons glace ginger,
chopped

2 tablespoons puffed quinoa

Makes about 16

Method

1. Preheat oven to 180°C (350°F) and line two large baking trays with non-stick baking paper.
2. Cream the butter with the coconut sugar until light and creamy then mix in the egg and vanilla.
3. Sift the quinoa flour with the ground ginger and baking powder, baking soda and fold into the creamed butter mixture.
4. Use a spatula to mix in the quinoa flakes, dates, ginger and quinoa puffs.
5. Spoon the mixture onto the prepared trays (one spoonful per cookie) and bake for about 10 minutes until golden.
6. Leave to cool slightly in trays before transferring to cooling rack to cool completely.
7. Store in an airtight container.

Carob Squares

Ingredients

90 g (3 oz) pure roasted
  carob powder
80 ml (2 fl oz) warm water
125 g (4 oz) butter
2 tablespoons golden syrup
  (maple syrup or honey)
1 teaspoon vanilla extract
45 g (1½ oz) puffed quinoa
45 g (1½ oz) slivered
  almonds
60 g (2 oz) dried sultanas
½ teaspoon ground
  cinnamon

Makes about 12

Method

1. Line the bottom of a 26 x 8 cm (10 x 3 inch) bar baking tin with non-stick baking paper and have the paper come up and overhang 2 sides to enable easy lift out of bars once they are ready.
2. Mix the carob powder and the water in a bowl and set aside.
3. Melt the butter in a small saucepan. Stir in the golden syrup then mix into the carob and water mixture with the vanilla.
4. Stir in the puffed quinoa, almonds, sultanas and cinnamon and mix until well combined and all the ingredients are totally covered.
5. Press the mixture down firmly into the prepared tin and refrigerate for at least 6 hours, preferably overnight, until set then cut into bars or slices to serve.

Note: Store these carob slices in the refrigerator in an airtight container. Carob is a great alternative to chocolate and most carob products are available at health food stores. They make a nice change from chocolate but make sure you use good quality pure carob powder. Raw cacao can be substituted for the carob powder and the golden syrup can be substituted with carob syrup. If using raw cacao, you may have to adjust the level of sweetness as raw cacao can be quite bitter.

Quinoa and Dried Fruit Yogurt Topping

Ingredients

4 tablespoons unsalted
   butter
3 tablespoons maple syrup
   or honey
2 tablespoons coconut sugar
1 teaspoon vanilla bean
   paste
125 g (4 oz) pitted Medjool
   dates, chopped into small
   pieces
4 tablespoons golden raisins
45 g (1½ oz) dried apricots,
   chopped
4 tablespoons puffed quinoa
unsweetened Greek yogurt
(or yogurt of choice), to
   serve

Makes about 750 g (27 oz)

Method

1. Preheat the oven to 160°C (325°F) and line a baking tray
    and line a baking tray with non-stick baking paper.
2. Melt butter in a small saucepan. Remove from heat and
    stir in the maple syrup, coconut sugar and vanilla. Set
    aside.
3. Place all other ingredients into a large bowl and mix well
    to combine with the butter mixture.
4. Spread the mixture on to the prepared tray and bake for
    about 20 minutes until golden.
5. Remove from the oven and leave to cool completely
    on the tray before removing and breaking up into small
    pieces.
6. Store in an airtight container and use as a topping with
    your favorite yogurt.

Maple Syrup, Coconut and Quinoa Cookies

—+···❁···+—

Ingredients

90 g (3 oz) quinoa flakes
3 tablespoons puffed quinoa
125 g (4 oz) quinoa flour
100 g (3½ oz) coconut sugar
1 teaspoon baking powder
1 teaspoon baking soda
    (bicarbonate soda)
75 g (2½ oz) shredded
    coconut
125 g (4 oz) butter, melted
2 tablespoons maple syrup
2 teaspoons vanilla extract
2 tablespoons hot water

Makes 20–24

Method

1. Preheat the oven to 160°C (325°F) and grease and line 2 baking trays with non-stick baking paper.
2. Place quinoa flakes, puffed quinoa, flour, coconut sugar, baking powder and baking soda into a bowl. Mix well then stir in the coconut.
3. Melt the butter then stir in the maple syrup, vanilla and hot water. Mix well.
4. Pour the melted butter mixture into the dry ingredients and mix until thoroughly combined.
5. Place spoonfuls of the cookie mixture onto prepared trays without overcrowding and bake for approximately 10 minutes until golden. Cool completely on the trays. The consistency should be soft when they come out of the oven and set as they cool.
6. Store in plastic container with a good fitting lid or a biscuit tin with a lid. They will last for about a week.

Note: These cookies can also be baked in different shapes. Place a cookie shape of choice on to the baking tray and press some of the cookie mixture into the shape. Carefully remove the cookie shape before baking.

Raw Cacao and Coconut Crackles

Ingredients

90 g (3 oz) puffed quinoa

3–4 tablespoons coconut sugar

4 tablespoons pure raw cacao powder

4 tablespoons shredded coconut

150 ml (5 fl oz) organic raw extra virgin coconut oil, melted

1 teaspoon vanilla

Makes about 24

Method

1. Place the puffed quinoa into a large bowl and mix in the coconut sugar making sure you break up any lumps.
2. Sift the cacao and add to the bowl then add the coconut and mix well.
3. Pour in the melted coconut oil. Add vanilla and mix until all ingredients are thoroughly combined and coated with the oil.
4. Spoon the mixture into patty cases and refrigerate until set. Store in the refrigerator in an airtight plastic container.

Note: If you would like a firmer set for these crackles, just add a little extra coconut oil.

These are great for children's parties although I must say that the big kids love them too. Start off with the lower amount of coconut sugar and taste and adjust to suit your taste. Keep in mind that the raw cacao is a little on the bitter side. You can make these in whatever size patty cases you wish. Organic raw extra virgin coconut oil is considered to be a superfood so these crackles are good for you.

Ice-Cream Balls

Ingredients

1 L (2 pt) good quality vanilla
    ice-cream
90 g (3 oz) almonds, skinned
45 g (1½ oz) puffed quinoa
2 tablespoons raw cacao
2 tablespoons maple syrup
1 teaspoon vanilla bean
    paste
fresh berries, to serve

Makes about 20

Method

1. Line a tray with non-stick baking paper and place into the freezer until it is really cold. If you can remember, place in the freezer days in advance so it is ready for you when you need it.
2. Remove the ice-cream from the freezer and allow it to melt enough so that you can put a spoon through it easily.
3. Place almonds into a non-stick frying pan and toast until golden. Remove from the pan and cool then roughly chop and set aside.
4. Place the puffed quinoa into a large non-stick frying pan in a single layer and toast lightly until golden. Keep an eye on the quinoa as they can burn easily. Keep tossing the pan to get an even toast. Set aside.
5. Place the ice-cream into a bowl and mix in the almonds, raw cacao, maple syrup and vanilla.
6. Return to the freezer and refreeze. When ice-cream is frozen again, take a scoop and roll in the toasted puffed quinoa. If the ice-cream is too solid, leave to defrost slightly before rolling in the quinoa.
7. Place the coated ice-cream balls onto the prepared icy-cold tray as you go and freeze until needed.
8. Once completely frozen, cover with plastic wrap or transfer to an airtight plastic container until needed.
9. Serve with fresh berries.

Note: You can use whatever nuts you like instead of the almonds. Brazil nuts or hazelnuts are a good substitute.

Rocky Road

—+···❆···+—

Ingredients

45 g (1½ oz) puffed quinoa

150 g (5 oz) marshmallows, small or large

60 g (2 oz) salted macadamias

30 g (1 oz) coconut flakes

100 g (3½ oz) red glace cherries

500 g (1 lb 1 oz) dark or milk chocolate

2 tablespoons coconut oil, melted

1 teaspoon vanilla bean paste

125 g (4 oz) white chocolate

Make 16–20 pieces

Method

1. Grease a 28 x 20 cm (11 x 8 inch) square deep dish and line the bottom and sides with non-stick baking paper.
2. Mix together the quinoa, marshmallows, macadamias, coconut and glace cherries. Set aside. Reserve some of the glace cherries and marshmallows for garnish.
3. Place chocolate in a bowl over a saucepan of simmering hot water and melt. When melted, stir in the coconut oil and vanilla then stir into the quinoa mix.
4. Pour into the prepared dish and set aside.
5. Melt the white chocolate over a saucepan of simmering water and then randomly place spoonfuls of the melted chocolate over the top of the dark chocolate mix.
6. Using a knife or wooden skewer, spread the white chocolate in a marbled effect through the mixture.
7. Garnish the top with the extra marshmallows and cherries and sprinkle some extra puffed quinoa over the top.
8. Refrigerate overnight until set then cut into desired sized pieces and enjoy.

INDEX

ACKNOWLEDGEMENTS

I would like to say a very special thank you to my dear friend and publisher, Linda Williams. Linda you have always been there for me— your advice and guidance has been invaluable.

To Fiona Schultz, Managing Director of New Holland, a special thank you for your continued support and encouragement in all my work. If it weren't for you and Linda and the trust you have shown in me from the very first book, none of the other books would have been possible.

A huge thank you to Victor Yoog from New Holland for his tireless work and help promoting my books. I have said this before, Victor, and I will say it again, nothing ever seems to be too much trouble for you; you're always more than willing to go out of your way. Your hard work has not gone unnoticed.

To my editor, Susie Stevens, and book designer, Lorena Susak, a huge thank you to both of you for taking my recipes and turning them into a beautiful book.

To Lucia Donnelly thank you so much for all the hard work and long hours that you put into publicizing my books in the media.

To the rest of the special team at New Holland, James Mills-Hicks, Jessica McNamara, Coral Khun, Olga Dementiev and all of the staff, thank you so much—you are all always so helpful and a pleasure to work with.

To two very important and talented people, my gorgeous photographer Sue Stubbs (our fifth book together, Sue) and stylist Imogene Roache, thank you both so much for making the photo shoot such a breeze and for bringing my recipes to life. Without the gorgeous photos and beautiful styling, this book would not be what it is.

Lastly to my wonderful and loving family: husband Graeme, my children Alex, Nikki and Christopher, their other halves Lachlan, Marcus and Carolyn and to my very precious grandchildren, Madison, Kobe, Isaac, Hudson and Cooper and to my parents thank you for your love and support always.

To our beautiful sweet Emma, miss you so much. The long hours spent on the computer working will never be the same again.

First published in 2016 by New Holland Publishers Pty Ltd
London • Sydney • Auckland

The Chandlery, Unit 704, 50 Westminster Bridge Road, London SE1 7QY United Kingdom
1/66 Gibbes Street, Chatswood NSW 2067 Australia
5/39 Woodside Avenue, Northcote, Auckland 0627 New Zealand

www.newhollandpublishers.com

A record of this book is held at the British Library and the National Library of Australia.

ISBN 9781742578217

Managing Director: Fiona Schultz
Publisher: Linda Williams
Project Editor: Susie Stevens
Designer: Lorena Susak
Photographer: Sue Stubbs
Food Stylist: Imogene Roache
Proofreader: Jessica McNamara
Production Director: James Mills-Hicks
Printer: Toppan Leefung Printing Limited

10 9 8 7 6 5 4 3 2 1

Keep up with New Holland Publishers on Facebook
www.facebook.com/NewHollandPublishers